Master/slave Mastery
ADVANCED

Refining the fire:
ideas that matter

Robert J. Rubel, Ph.D.
with M. Jen Fairfield

Master/slave Mastery
ADVANCED

Refining the fire:
ideas that matter

Robert J. Rubel, Ph.D.
with M. Jen Fairfield

Red 8 Ball
Press

www.KinkMastery.com

Red Eight Ball Press
P.O. Box 171303
Austin, TX 78717

Master/slave Mastery—
Advanced
refining the fire, ideas that matter
© 2015 by Robert J. Rubel and M. Jen Fairfield

ISBN 978-0-9863521-6-4

Cover Design: Robert Rubel
Layout: Andrea Rhodes

Library of Congress Catalog Number: 2015949164

Published by Red Eight Ball Press
Austin, Texas

Printed in the United States of America

www.KinkMastery.com

Dedication

This book is dedicated to Master Skip Chasey; he changed my life.

Master Skip Chasey was in Austin in the summer of 2003 conducting a weekend intensive on spirituality in Leather. Our club assigned him to stay at my home. I had never heard of him, and "Leather" was only occasionally mentioned in our local club. I had two years of BDSM experience; I had no idea who this man was.

At our home in the evenings, we would talk. He asked questions; he led me to ask questions. The ideas were new. I realized I'd stumbled into an area of my own unconscious incompetence: I didn't know what I didn't know. More than new, much of what Master Skip was saying came from a different universe than I lived in. He was so eloquent…

I committed myself to learning about the Leather lifestyle. Within a year, I began to turn away from BDSM and towards my understanding of the Leather Master/slave culture. Within a year, I had both an Owner and a slave.

As I began attending conferences, I also started attending his workshops. It seemed that Master Skip was a presenter at virtually every conference I attended. We were seeing one another three or four times a year. I made it a point to attend his classes. Over the years, much of my own thinking has resulted from Master Skip's wise observations. In fact, I have over 20 of his concepts/ideas included this book.

I have attended over 60 weekend BDSM or Leather conferences spanning nearly 15 years. With confidence, I will say that Master Skip Chasey has had among the greatest impact on our community of any single individual.

I particularly thank Master Skip for permitting me to use part of the title of one of his early workshops for part of this book's title. His class, "Refining Fire: The Role of sm in Master/slave Relationships." (South Plains Leatherfest, 2004) affected me profoundly. I have referenced many of the 10 points from his class handout in most of the books I've written on the subject of Master/slave relationships.

This community has repeatedly recognized him for his overall contributions; I now add mine.

Master Skip, thank you for being my friend and thank you for being an inspiration to so many of us.

Master/slave Mastery
ADVANCED

*Refining the fire:
ideas that matter*

Foreword

If you have purchased this book in order to try to *understand* why people become involved with a Master/slave dynamic, you may be disappointed. Many of us feel it to be a *calling. Reason* and *understanding* may not help much when one feels *called* to something. Some people enter M/s structures for reasons that defy rational explanation. People both gain and lose life-long friends when they follow their heart and become a Master or a slave.

This book is as much about philosophy (mind-set) as it is about the *doing* of M/s. Perhaps because I've discovered so many of the truths included here only after living and studying Master/slave relationships, I've become a bit strident.

I'm not meaning to provide a general model of M/s, I'm meaning to open your mind to some of the underlying principles. While there may not be "one true way" to do Master/slave relationships, there is, in fact, very close to "one true way" to lead an ethical and honorable life that supports you as you hone your personal Mastery.

Purposefully structured relationships are *communication-rich.* You both have done a lot of talking to get to this place. When couples pre-negotiate their power dynamic, most of the upset and fighting seen in more traditional relationships is removed. That makes authority-imbalanced relationships particularly effective and stable.

Of course, this model presumes the Master knows how to lead, the slave is willing to obey, and all this is carried out within the context of a rigorously ethical relationship.

To start you thinking, here are three resources typical of those I'll list throughout this book:
- *The 7 Habits of Highly Effective People* by Stephen Covey
- *Mastery* by Robert Greene
- *The Tipping Point: How Little Things Can Make a Big Difference* by Malcolm Gladwell

Foreword

From Stephen Covey, I offer you his observation that there are two different cultural approaches to how you lead your life. He calls one approach *the character ethic.* He calls the other approach *the personality ethic.* Character ethic is based on outward actions and on core values such as honor, integrity, loyalty, and trust. Personality ethic is based on *looking* the part rather than *being* the part; on dressing well, standing with good posture, knowing the "in" words, phrases, and such.

From Robert Greene, I offer you a work that can serve as your personal roadmap to master whatever you choose. Using countless examples from history, Greene distills the kernels of truth and meaning you can apply personally.

From Malcolm Gladwell, I offer you a statistic: to become very good at something you have to have logged over 5,000 hours of active practice; to become an expert at something, you have to have spent over 10,000 hours of active practice. Some things to think about.

Mastery is a serious business and I take it seriously. This is meant as a serious book.

In 2006, I published a book titled: *Master/slave Relations: Handbook of Theory and Practice.* I began presenting at national conferences throughout the U.S. in 2007. Between 2007 and 2015, I conservatively estimate I've presented on Master/slave topics at over 80 conferences and for about 20 two-day "weekend intensives." Presenters are generally asked to make two presentations per conference. If you conservatively estimate that 25 people attend each class, I've spoken before something like 4,000 people. That's without considering the countless people with whom I speak while selling my books at these conferences.

Now, I generally am able to attend one or two workshops at each conference where I am a presenter or contest judge. Mostly, I go to classes on Master/slave topics of one kind or another. Thus, over these years I've attended something like 80 x 1.5 workshops: 120 presentations, more-or-less. I learned from those with whom I spoke. As an inveterate note-taker I have a substantial collection of workshop notes.

I'm mentioning all this to give you a context for this book.

This book is a collection of my own material plus interesting ideas picked up at weekend conference classes going back to 2003. I've also included notes taken while speaking with those who attended my classes. This is the second book in our Master/slave Mastery series. The first book is designed to prepare readers for this book; it's more challenging.

I hope you gain as much knowledge reading this book as I have during the writing of it.

A servant serves Master's needs or is fired;
a slave serves Master's wants or is released.

However, Master's wants must not trump slave's needs,
even when playing by RACK standards.

slave is in service to Master;
However, Master is in service to the relationship.

Welcome to the complex and elegant
world of Master/slave relations.

Table of Contents

Introduction: Not for Beginners

Sometimes, wisdom comes to you quite suddenly. Sometimes it comes from something someone says. Sometimes it comes from something you read. I hope this book adds to your wisdom.

If I don't miss my guess, you bought this book because you're curious. That wasn't too tough to guess, was it? After all, why *else* would you buy a book? Oh, in order to speak with you directly, I write in the first-person present tense. Welcome to my world. Come in and pull up a chair. Let's talk.

I repeat: why did you buy this book? If it were I, **I** certainly would have bought this book because I was curious. I'd have been curious what someone else has to say about what I consider to be a complex kind of relationship with which I'm very familiar. So, if you know enough to have bought this book out of curiosity, I'd also guess you're heavily involved with an authority-imbalanced relationship and, like many of us, you grab at anything that looks promising. I hope I don't disappoint.

And, let me be clear: if, as you read this book, you take exception to some parts, or you have ideas that could expand the next edition, please write to me. I'm very accessible through www.KinkMastery. com. If you participate in Fetlife, I'm Dr_Bob: feel free to send me a friend request.

Introduction

This is an advanced book for those of us who are fascinated by what two (or more) people can do with an authority-imbalanced relationship. These sorts of relationships can be *edgy* because they usually involve more personal emotional risk than boyfriend/girlfriend or husband/wife structures. Most of us who live this way have grown accustomed to constantly monitoring and evaluating not only our partner's actions/reactions, but also our own response to their behaviors. For many of us, "relationships" are our kink—we're sort-of *relationship geeks.*

In addition to being a relationship geek, I'm personally a *relationship knowledge* geek. Over the years, I've been fascinated by the little tidbits of knowledge I've picked up from speaking with other Masters and slaves, from reading books, from attending challenging workshops at Master/slave conferences, and speaking with countless fascinating people about what we do and how we live.

I've always enjoyed being exposed to new ideas and concepts. I am intrigued to discover seemingly simple ideas that somehow had never before occurred to me. While some of these ideas were so uncomplicated they only needed pointing out, others that at first appeared reasonably straightforward turned out to be so complex they required years of thought (and many pages of writing) to develop their full flavor and richness. So it has been with Master/slave structures. They *seemed* so simple.

> As you read, keep this in mind:
>
> Writing is an abstraction of our speech,
> Which is an abstraction of our thinking,
> Which is an abstraction of our culture.

Look: I'm trying to expose you to a range of ideas. Some ideas will be new to you; some won't be so new. Regardless, these ideas are among the best I've gleaned after many years of study and thought about the subject of consensual authority-imbalanced relationships. I'm offering them to you in the spirit of David Hume, who said: "All knowledge resolves itself into probability." I hope this book increases your probability of turning your M/s relationship into something spectacular. I congratulate you if your relationship is already sensational; please consider that it could become even better.

Why Master/slave?

In my view, the Master/slave dynamic provides a creative and flexible opportunity for like-minded people to design a magical life for themselves… as long as their purposes and intentions are aligned. When you find a strong, visionary leader coupled with a strong supportive follower, quite a bit can happen. However, this formula of interconnected service and support is contrary to the Master/slave dynamic often expressed in fiction. In most M/s fiction, the slave simply does as Master instructs because that's the way it is. This approach will work for a while, but after some years, it may spawn problems if Master and slave do not retain the same intention. The slave may feel their life is being thrown away fulfilling someone else's dream. They may feel trapped, bitter, and angry.

I assert it's possible to get more out of your M/s relationship than most vanillas get out of their marriages. The catch: Master must be actively aware they are 100% responsible for slave's emotional, physical, social, financial and spiritual, well being.

Right, you know that and I know you know that. But, do you *act* upon that knowledge? As Master, are you careful to hold your own emotions in check as you strive to understand what the slave is expressing as a need? Are you even-handed in ensuring you are meeting your slave's needs as much as your slave strives to meet your wants? Have you clearly communicated to slave the growth path on which you have set them?

I'm bringing this up because mismatches can creep up on you, even in established relationships. As life rolls along, an M/s couple can be surprised to find their relationship has drifted away from how it was to something much more mundane. Master's leadership slackens as familiarity sets in; slave's service slackens as they focus on getting through the day (in contrast to serving Master's will throughout the day).

Again, if you believe you remain in harmony, everything's fine. If you suspect there could be room for improvement, then read on.

Mismatches between your individual needs of the overall relationship can occur for many reasons. First, Master and slave may not put the same priority on the relationship's needs. Second, their priorities may have changed as the relationship matured. Third, they may not have ever tried to prioritize their understanding of one another's needs. Fourth, it took an upset for differences between the way Master and slave rank relationship needs to become revealed. That brings me back to suggest you sit down and work together to rank-order your respective needs to avoid accidental mismatches.

People are strongly inclined to get their needs met, whether you're speaking of kink needs, emotional needs, psycho/social needs, sexual needs, or survival needs ("survival" meaning social survival every bit as much as it means a roof over your head and food and sanitation facilities). Just think about it: at the extremes, both Master and slave have the ethical requirement to step aside from a relationship where one partner can't meet the other partner's stated need(s). I'll even personalize this: within my current relationship with Master, this boy realizes if he develops Alzheimer's or some other mental condition, it is honor-bound to leave its Master, for Master has been clear from the outset we have a cerebrally-based relationship and she is not going to be able to live with someone who isn't mentally acute. I get it.

Let's make sure we're on the same page

Relationships struggle – they all will at some point.

Master/slave relationships can be fairly simple or extremely complex. It rather depends on your own personalities and your purpose for being in this kind of relationship structure. M/s relationships are whatever you make of them; some last for a few months, others go on for decades.

Like couples of all persuasions, M/s couples start out in lustful passion but slow down as the daily reality of living M/s takes over. Once the new-and-sparkly phase ends, the couple has to manage this relationship in a real way. In this new reality, the quality of Master's guidance is reflected by the degree of the slave's contentment. A risk arises: after a few months, Master may not be quite so keen on directing slave's diet, exercise, skin care, and grooming. Or, in an effort to bend the slave to their will, Master may find themselves being more domineering than dominant.

Another potential struggle can arise after a few months and slave has learned all Master wishes slave to learn. The opportunities offered at the beginning of the relationship, the opportunities for Master to teach and for slave to learn, are no longer necessary. slave's actions appear not to be noticed by Master as "correction" is no longer necessary. A relationship that began with a lot of focus on protocols may struggle from the loss of focus once protocols become routine (and invisible to Master).

Resentment can set in on both sides of the slash. Master may not have realized the amount of work involved in keeping this dream going; slave may feel their own needs are being bypassed in favor of Master's needs, and they didn't think that was *really* the deal.

Many people simply break up at this point and try starting over with another person. That probably won't work very well, for reasons described in this book.

The trouble with using experience as a guide is that the final exam often comes first…

and then the lesson.

While we will experience struggles within our relationships – this book is not about those struggles. This book is written to remind us to use different tools and different ideas to help us keep our relationships feeling new and sparkly.

The author's mindset

639 words about Asperger Syndrome

Some "messy relationships" are hard to clean up.

Something like one in 250 people falls somewhere on the *Autism Spectrum Disorder* scale. That's the current phrase for Asperger Syndrome, also known as "high-end autism." I'm inserting this discussion here, because the following section is about "love in service-based relationships" and *love* and *relationships* can be blown to Hell for any number of reasons, including when one partner is an Aspie—as I am. It's suspected to be hereditary and manifests mostly in men.

Autism Spectrum Disorder (ASD) affects their ability to understand and respond to others' thoughts and feelings. The person may *appear* to be normal—and even be successful in work and in life—but just seem a little *off* in some situations. AS is a "brain wiring" issue: our brain wiring is a little different than you commonly encounter. The most general description is of a person who is unusually articulate and unusually socially inept.

Aspie characteristics can be confusing and hurtful. They don't play out well in relationships. Here's a quick overview of a few common symptoms as they particularly affect *me:*

- **Facial expressions:** I have trouble interpreting facial expressions (called *mind-blindness)*. During conversations, I am mostly *taking in* the words and missing the emotions expressed by the person's face. (It also means it's hard to connect names with faces, a constant embarrassment at BDSM conferences when I'm meeting someone for the fifth time whom I've never "seen" before.)
- **Subtlety:** I seldom understand subtlety: people have to be particularly direct with me—I don't even realize I've missed the point (Jen often has to interpret the subplot of movies to me, particularly romantic movies and dramas—I just don't get it).
- **Focus:** I become very focused when working on something. Although I'll reply if someone interrupts me with a question, I'm not likely to be able to recall the conversation 10-20 minutes later.

- **Confusion:** Clashes in thinking styles can make it hard for me to *understand* some people—and I won't even realize we are not communicating effectively. They say "X" and I hear and act on "stone." Often, I'm not even in the same book, let alone the same page. This tends to make people angry with me, for they think either I'm toying with them or insulting them.
- **Empathy:** Because I find it difficult to "put myself into the shoes" of another person, I tend not to understand the impact of what I'm saying; I tend not to appreciate what others are going through in their lives.

Attention Deficit Disorder (ADD) usually accompanies the Asperger diagnosis. Here's a cute description of ADD. It's from a T-shirt logo I saw one time: "Attention Deficit—Oh Look!! A squirrel!"

I'm bringing this up because most people assume others think as they do. They probably don't. Obviously, undiagnosed psychological conditions can complicate relationships. If some of your partner's reactions seem a bit unusual, consider some cognitive testing. I recommend you start by taking a Myers-Briggs test. They're free and easy to find. Then, do an Internet search to compare how the two (or more) of you are likely to interact. This can be an eye-opener.

I was first told I probably had Asperger Syndrome in 2006: I was 62: it was confirmed by testing two years later. That means my partners from the time I was 28 (first married) to 62 have had to put up with a lot of often-hurtful behavior beyond my own understanding.

All of which leads me to share some important points:
- We must overcome the notion that we must be regular...it robs us of the chance to be extraordinary and leads us to the mediocre. [Uta Hagen]
- Leadership is action, not position. [Donald H. McGannon]
- In the long run, it's more orderly to convert chaos to system than to cover chaos with system. [Stephen Gilbert, Planning for the Future, 1973]
- Master's wants may trump slave's wants but must not trump slave's needs. [Karen Cupp, author of *How to Capture a Mistress*]

And with that, we begin the book.

Scope of the book

This book presents my views on life and relationships. Some of my views evolved from the dozens of M/s workshops I've attended; others, come from non-kink relationship and communication books I've read and courses I've taken. My views also evolved from personally living in structured M/s relationships since 2003. I lived as property for ten years, as Master concurrently during eight of those ten years, and currently as slave. I am a psychological switch, but you would know that simply from the prior sentence.

In writing this book, I've assumed you've had more than five years of experience in your structure, or you've already read the first book in our "Master/slave Mastery" series—the book called: *Master/slave Mastery: Updated handbook of concepts, approaches, and practices.* If you haven't, you may find this book a little hard to grasp. It's not for beginners.

"There are many paths to the top of the mountain, but the view from the top is the same no matter how you get there. If you can see the path in front of you, you're probably following someone else's path."

—Master Skip Chasey

I believe the more senior you are in the M/s world, the more fun it will be to read this book. This doesn't mean you'll agree with everything in here; it only means you'll understand this material in the context of your own experiences.

Submissive and slave—some prefatory notes

I'll begin by proposing that "submissive" and "slave" motivations and behaviors aren't quite the same. While one is certainly not better than the other, one set of behaviors is more likely to fit some people than others. At the most fundamental level, one tends to speak about "having" a submissive versus "owning" a slave. This, itself, is a window into the profound differences between the two.

Although the descriptions I'm about to provide may appear to be neat and clean, it's not this way in real life. Some slaves identify as *submissives* even though they have surrendered authority over themselves to their Dom/me. While they refer to themselves as *submissives*, their relationship structure appears objectively to be closer to "slave" than to "sub." Similarly, the Dom/mes in control of such slaves may not consistently refer to themselves as "Master." This rich complexity of relationship structures and roles—this land of flexibility and possibility— makes the BDSM world hard to understand yet lots of fun to live in.

Here is my version of a graduate-school level synopsis of this discussion: "Dominant" and "submissive" describe ways people display their personality in various settings. The words "slave" or "property" describes roles one can assume whether one is displaying dominance or submission.

Said another way, a "slave" or "property" are not personality descriptors; those words describe roles within a relationship. The personality of the slave or the property is a separate discussion from their role. Someone with a dominant personality can be as much of a slave as someone with a submissive personality. Just think about slaves in an historical sense. Can you imagine a slave trader saying: "Oh, you're too dominant to be a good slave; you're free to go." Silly.

In our modern version of Master/slave, the determining factor is this: the person filling the slave role chose to do so. The fact someone chooses to be a slave does not make them "submissive" any more than a heterosexual man choosing to have anal sex makes him gay.

By the way, if you want to see a really clean version of a strong dominant who has put himself into service of an even stronger female Master, consider watching the movie titled: *The Young Victoria* on Amazon. The last 10 minutes are very telling. Prince Albert was hardly a submissive.

In my world, the *behaviors* and *actions* of a person filling the "submissive" role in a D/s structure can be almost indistinguishable from a person filling the "slave" role in an M/s structure. Nevertheless, there are important differences: First, while the *submissive* has the authority to negotiate areas where they retain some degree of personal authority and control, the slave does not. Second, D/s structures tend to have far fewer (and less formal) protocols than M/s structures. Third, unlike D/s structures, M/s structures tend to start out with contracts between the two parties, beginning the relationship with forethought. Fourth, an M/s "Master" is usually judged more by their leadership abilities than by their "masculine dominant" characteristics.

Submissives and slaves are individuals, and individuals differ in countless ways. Relationships differ, as does our conduct within each relationship. Whether one considers oneself to be a "submissive," a "slave," or "property" is a matter of personal choice mixed with loosely observed definitions.

In the following chapter I'll demonstrate what can happen when you combine these various characteristics into relationship structures.

Now, a high-level reality check
Here are some of my own views. They form the foundation of my thinking and of this book. You may or may not share these beliefs— at least not right now. However, you've only just begun reading. These views, and the reasons they are my views, will be woven throughout this book.

Since the following statements represent the assumptions underlying all my writing, I thought I'd lay them out all in one place.
- **M/s ≠ BDSM, part one:** Sexual sado-masochistic practices are not relevant to the way we'll be discussing structured relationships in this book. This is a relationships book, and sex practices are outside its scope.
- **M/s ≠ BDSM, part two:** In M/s, the focus is on **relationships**; in BDSM, the focus is on sm **activities**. More than this, BDSM is a *conversation* not a description, as my friend Bob Ritchey (Bydarra on Fet) puts it.
- **M/s ≠ D/s, part one:** I'll not be discussing whether a Master is or is not a dominant. In my view, dominance and submission are aspects of one's personality and Mastery and slavery are

about roles and behaviors.

- **M/s ≠ D/s, part two:** Slightly edited to match the tone of this book, this material comes from a particularly astute and thoughtful essay by J.M. Togneri (Fet = LordSpooner) in his article, "Absolute Misunderstanding" available on www.leathernroses.com.
    - The actual D/s dynamic is quite fluid for most couples. They can choose among various types and intensities of dominance and submission—even to the point of shifting between them. D/s is based on power "exchange": *Exchange* requires discussion and negotiation, a giving and receiving. In D/s structures, the submissive retains some degree of personal authority over him/herself: in M/s, the slave has surrendered personal autonomy and in many/most M/s relationships, would have to ask its Master for authority to carry out many normal daily functions.
    - The M/s dynamic is a symbiosis, not an exchange: it is a host/parasite relationship in which both are simultaneously host and parasite to one another. To a greater or lesser degree, each symbiont provides something the other needs, but does so passively, merely by existing—indeed sometimes as a by-product of the very action of getting what it itself needs. The key point, here, is that it is *not* an exchange, it's a *melding*. The M/s couple view themselves as speaking with one voice. (Symbiosis takes three forms: *mutualism*, where both the symbiont and host benefit; *commensalism*, where the symbiont benefits with little effect on the host; and *parasitism*, where the symbiont benefits to the detriment of the host. You'll find all three alive and well among M/s couples you meet.)
- **M/s ≠ D/s, part three:** The need to *submit* = D/s; the need to *serve* = M/s.
- **M/s ≠ D/s, part four:** M/s involves leadership authority; D/s involves managing control.
- **slave** vs. **servant:** slaves do what others want, servants do what others need. Key concept: if the paid servant doesn't do

what is needed, they are fired.

- **Obedience ≠ submission:** Obedience is external; submission is internal. Obedience is an action; submission is an internal force. You can obey all day long due to outside control (speed limits, your boss, societal norms, etc.), but *submitting* to someone comes from an internal desire to give up control.
- **Do** vs. **have:** In M/s we *do* a relationship, it comes from our being; it's part of us. We don't *have* a relationship, *having* is possession and is a passive act. M/s relationships are moment-by-moment, daily, wholly consuming: they are *who we are.*
- SM is what we do = **sex;** "Leather" (or some other construct) is who we are = what we believe in = **values;** M/s is how we interrelate = **relationship** = **families.**
- *To serve* doesn't always mean *to follow*; sometimes it means *to lead*.
- There is a big difference between Mastering through **love** (boyfriend/girlfriend) vs. Mastering through **power** (D/s) vs. Mastering through the **authority** (M/s) daily granted by the slave who has *chosen* to follow their Master.
- I agree with Tristan Taormino: BDSMers are really "sex geeks." BDSMers study SM skills to augment their sexual lives. I would extend this analogy and say that those of us practicing 24/7 M/s are "relationship geeks." We study leadership styles, relationship issues and various approaches to self-mastery in order to improve our relationships.
- **"Leather"** and **"Not-Leather":** This book is written from the heterosexual "Leather" perspective. If you find yourself saying, "Gosh, this isn't true in my experience," that's fine—people's experiences are different. I can only write from my own experience.
- Recognition often comes through public ceremony. One *becomes* a Master; one doesn't start out that way any more than a raw military recruit starts out as a Major.

Why we keep doing this

According to the *Annual Review of Sociology,* within five years of moving in together fifty-five percent of cohabitant couples get married and forty percent break up. And… those are vanilla relationships—a walk in the park compared with our more radical authority-imbalanced relationships.

When it comes to M/s relationships, it can be challenging to get the right fit—even when both parties seem to be plenty smart and lustily willing. Cracks can appear in the aging painting of the two of you: you're not yet *alarmed,* but all is not peaches and cream. It's turned out that…

- Either Master or slave didn't bring enough to the table (e.g. not enough physical or interpersonal skills and/or not enough leader/follower wisdom/knowledge).
- Master is inconsistent in handling the slave; slave doesn't seem able to work through (or solve) problems the way Master wishes.
- Over the years together, one or both of you have changed and your current "wants" are no longer what you thought you had initially wanted from this relationship. You now find yourselves in a committed relationship with misaligned goals.

Regardless of the way you structure your relationship or the reasons the two (or more) of you are together, I believe the control and structure of M/s affords us two great opportunities. First, it enables us to grow in self-understanding; second, it affords us the opportunity to learn ways to create a spectacular relationship. Unfortunately, there's a catch (there *always* is a catch, you know): you must *choose* to want to create a spectacular relationship. The good news is this: if you choose it, and act upon that choice, you have an opportunity to create an extremely gratifying relationship. You can create a relationship that is a daily celebration of life. The bad news: you must both choose and *act.* Choose and act. A dream fulfilled is a choice acted upon.

It takes a tremendous amount of commitment and work to craft and maintain a spectacular Master/slave relationship. That's why many of us consider it to be a *calling.* We are willing to put in the time and the work because we just couldn't live any other way.

This book is intended to give you ideas to get you thinking about your Mastery or slavery.

That's all a book can do.

.

Chapter 1: Relationships

M/s relationships can be confusing to others because it is a non-traditional relationship structure. Others don't quite know how to behave around a couple where one partner claims to own the other. Sometimes, we, ourselves, get confused about it.

The second edition of the Oxford English Dictionary defines "slave" thus: "One who is the property of—and entirely subject to—another person, whether by capture, purchase or birth; a servant completely divested of freedom and personal rights."

You can parse it one way or dice it another way; you can blend it until it's a muddled grey, or you can look it straight in the eye: The cleanest way to divide Master/slave relationships from other kinds of D/s relationships is this: the slave is consensually owned property. After all, throughout recorded history, what else were marauding armies securing when they captured people? Property: wealth.

Now: people who don't like the "slave" word will go nuts with that paragraph, but at some point you have to call it what it is, and that's what it is. Our culture isn't endangered because some minuscule percentage of the U.S. population is comfortable in this kind of setting; we're not looking for converts.

Chapter 1: Relationships

Actually, when you think about it, more than anything, M/s relationships are a complex and sophisticated way to be very clear about what you want for yourself and your partner—accompanied by a plan of action. No, not everybody takes advantage of these aspects of a structured relationship, but not everybody takes advantage of *anything.*

This raises a pivotal point: as Master, you've captured wealth. This leads to the follow-on question: are you able to make your wealth grow or will you squander it?

It's up to each Master to determine what it means to "own" another person. It's also up to each Master to define what "to grow your slave" even means. My personal approach is to be thoughtful and purposeful. I use this structure as a vehicle to learn more about myself and to make changes where my evolving moral/ethical code directs me. However, I'm fairly cerebral.

For others, it's just plane fun to go against societal norms in this way. And for still others, it's... (So: can you express clearly why you're doing M/s?)

Most of us who choose to serve another person in this fashion maintain a simple mental attitude: we no longer own anything or control what used to be our money and our time. In fact, for many of us, whether or not Master returns our affection rather misses the point: we're doing this for our own unique reasons. Many of us have decided we're here on Earth to serve and to obey this particular person. Our common credo is: "Follow directions and take what you get." For many, this is a freeing perspective. Speaking purely personally, this gives me creative freedom. As our Family is devoted to education and learning, I no longer have to anguish over whether or not I'm appropriately caring for and nurturing a slave. Now, I only have to attend to Master's wants and needs. My days are filled with serving Master or writing—with a little time out to go to work at an office.

Obviously, people start down the Master/slave Path for all kinds of reasons. The popular masculine "porn version" of M/s is that slave has two choices: obey or be punished. Repeated disobedience results in being released. The motto of this camp is: "The first time you mess up, shame on you; the second time you mess up, shame on me; the third time you mess up you're dismissed from service." After all, goes this line of thought, there is an endless supply of potential slaves. In this model, slave has bonded heavily with Master, but the Master does **not** reflect the same level of bonding (commitment) to the slave. Master is primarily committed to living in a relationship structure where his/her wants are fulfilled and will be as little involved with the slave as possible so long as the slave continues to serve the Master's wants. It's not the person; it's the service. Many slaves will only figure this out after living in structure for many years.

The troubles with this perspective are legion, but for starters, it leads to a lot of heartbreak when it collides with the popular fantasy model of slavery: to be possessed by a strong dominant Master and be protected for the rest of their lives. Hmmm: very different assumptions.

Later in this chapter I'll revisit this conflict between assumptions in the section titled: "*To own* versus *to possess.*"

Structure fits the people

Structured relationships seem to come in two basic flavors: **power-imbalanced** relationships, and **authority-imbalanced** relationship. The power-imbalanced group ranges from "soft D/s" such as Daddy/girl) to "extreme D/s" or TPE—Total Power Exchange. The authority-imbalanced group lives somewhere along the Master/slave or Owner/property continuum.

Or so it seems to me, after studying it for some time.

It might help if I expand this thought a bit more.

Some background

You don't know what you don't know.
Maintaining a healthy M/s relationship isn't quite as easy as it might at first appear. I've discussed this topic with many Masters, and many

have shared their stories with me. While some of their stories were more revealing than others, my overall sense confirms simple logic: some did better than others. Some Masters did a little damage; some did a lot. None got it right from the beginning—after all, how could they? Many admitted that when they started down this Path, they misused their powers as a "slave owner." Interestingly, they mostly attributed their stumbles to lack of access to information about living in an authority-imbalanced relationship. That's hard to imagine, as there are many authors writing about this and related topics. However, not much was written in the 1970-90 period, and certainly nothing about heterosexual Master/slave relationship structures.

In all likelihood, the idea about role-playing "Master/slave" began as a gay barroom pickup line: "Master, take me home and I'll be your slave: do whatever you want with me!" Only after books such as *The Story of O*, *The Marketplace* trilogy, and the *Gor* novels did the general public get the idea they might be able to pull this off in real time.

When M/s started—no, I'm not going to be so foolish as to give any years—there were no models to follow nor books read: people experimented and did the best they could. The results were rather like what you'd get by throwing a handful of confetti into the air—some relationship strategies worked out; others didn't. Experimentation led to some of the figurative confetti clumping together in one pile or another. Over time, a few "schools of thought" began to emerge about how to "do" M/s. Now, those who read these books and attend educational programs about D/s and M/s relationships have a distinct advantage on those who try to make it up as they go along.

Taking the larger view, M/s has gone from a gay barroom scene leading to hot Leathersex ("Leather" became a euphemism for "rough sex") to a descriptor (of some sort) for a kind of extremely-non-traditional 24/7 relationship where one person "owns" another.

Hmmm. That's a leap. Let me keep pushing the point…

This is not the book for players or M/s beginners
Not meaning to speak shorthand, but D/s and M/s represent relationship tags with substantially different meanings…

Dominant and *submissive* are personality descriptors, not role descriptors. *Master* and *slave* are role descriptors, not personality descriptors. This is a fundamental distinction, and it makes it easier to understand how a Master can have a slave who is Master to another slave (as I lived for eight years).

This is your book if you're experienced in M/s. If you're not so experienced, you might consider first reading some more basic books. I've written this book for people who go to Master/slave weekend conferences and have already read quite a bit on the subject. Oh, on the subject of reading, I've included some book suggestions in the Supplements.

Certainly, there are different *levels of engagement* among M/s couples. Some couples "scene" M/s as a bedroom activity (because they have children still living at home). Other couples can only be "in structure" on weekends when they feel they are able to set "real life" aside and have better focus to give to their relationship. Still other people have a part-time or long-distance M/s relationship where Master's control is uneven. I suspect most reading this book live 24/7 where Master has total authority over slave.

By the way, in last paragraph I said Master has "authority over...." In this level of relationship, Master most often is said to have "authority" over the slave rather than "control" over the slave. "Control" is more commonly found in D/s relationships where discipline and punishment are woven into the relationship's fabric. Here, because one has such authority there is seldom need for control—the slave is, after all, in voluntary service to you and has pledged to obey you. What do you need *control* for? This underlying theme is interlaced throughout this book.

Growing interest in structured relationships

Interest in structured relationships has grown dramatically in recent years. As a measure, just look at the growth of local MAsT Chapters (Masters And slaves Together). Here are the stats showing the number of chapters per year and overall MAsT membership according to (and with thanks to) Master Bob Blount (former Executive Director of MAsT International and MzSusan, the current Executive Director):

Chapter 1: Relationships

Year	Number of Chapters	Total MAsT Membership
2007	38	700
2008	49	784
2009	67	1,206
2010	76	1,396
2011	86	1,550
2012	112	2,552
2013	110	2,980
2014	120	3,160

Distinguishing between D/s and M/s

Despite the BDSM sense that D/s *play* is time-limited, we frequently see long-lasting relationships grow to incorporate *negotiated D/s*. In fact, many see power exchange relationships as an effective way for two or more people to choose well-defined roles for themselves and their partner(s). There is a dominant partner who has leadership responsibility and there is a submissive partner (or two) whose responsibilities include both preserving harmony and supporting the D-type. The two (or more) work out ways their individual abilities can best meet their common needs. D/s structures generally afford more leeway, more give-and-take than M/s structures.

There are a number of overlapping elements between D/s and M/s relationships, and it can be hard to tell them apart. Often, you'll have to ask the Master how they refer to their particular structure.

Characteristics shared both by D/s and M/s relationships
- The roles of each partner have been pre-negotiated and there is an agreed-upon leader and follower.
- Most of the relationship parameters have been pre-negotiated and there are stated rules of behavior.
- There are consequences within the relationship for failure to comply with those rules.

- One person serves the wants/needs of the other.
- One person generally checks in with the other before doing things
- The person who has the role of being "in charge" must exhibit above-average ethical and leadership behaviors so their partner will continue to serve.

Characteristics more common in D/s structures:
- Dominance is a key characteristic of the relationship.
- Amorous love (*Eros*) and friendship (*philia*) are more of the focus than spiritual love (*Agape*)
- Master Skip Chasey refers to D/s as "about the mental body."

Characteristics more common in M/s structures:
- Possibly due to their complexity M/s structures often involve a written contract to help define terms of the "offer" and "acceptance."
- Master is 100% responsible for all aspects of the slave's well-being—mental health, physical health, finances, etc.
- The emphasis in the relationship is on *growth*. Master is either "growing a slave or growing a man" to use Master Skip Chasey's phrasing in the book edited by David Stein titled: *Ask the Man Who Owns Him.* Master Skip is suggesting that in one case, the slave is intended to remain in personal service to the Master, while in the other case, both the Master and slave recognize early on (perhaps from the start) that the Master is mentoring/training role the slave who will move on after the course is completed (perhaps to be a Master in their own right).
- Psychological dominance is not a requirement; ethical leadership is a requirement.
- Spiritual love (*Agape*) and friendship (*philia*) are more of the focus than amorous love (*Eros*).
- Most M/s structures stress the ethical code expressed as HILT: honor, integrity, loyalty, and trust. Words such as "focus," "purpose," and "intent" are common M/s topics.
- Master Skip Chasey refers to M/s as "about the spiritual body." For the many of us who use the M/s dynamic for spiritual connection, the greatest challenge for the slave is what is called "ego surrender" (See: Raven Kaldera's book *Sacred Power* for more on this topic). Please refer to the Supplement for resources

to help you further explore this area. This is advanced material and not appropriate for this book.

- M/s practitioners often refer to their relationship as a "Family" and often have extended Family members who are part of the House.

Few authority-imbalanced relationships look alike. Yes, you can make some general observations about various structures, but individual needs, preferences, and dreams produce unique results. This is an area where styles of leadership combine with styles of teaching and learning and blend with personal preferences to create relationships that may be called one thing but look like another thing.

What one couple calls D/s someone else may call M/s. What another couple calls M/s someone else may call O/p (Owner/property) or TPE (Total Power Exchange). You are the only people who care how you name your structure. As an author, my role is to force some definitions in this book so you'll know what I mean when I use those words or terms.

As you learn more about structured relationships, you will learn these can be very sophisticated arrangements. For many, Master is serving the slave's needs every bit as much as the slave is fulfilling Master's wants. To paraphrase Master Ron K in his essay: "On Becoming More…" in Raven Kaldera's book *Sacred Power:* the slave meets the Master's desires while the Master meets the slave's needs.

Distinguishing between O/p and M/s
Over the last few years there has been a tendency to distinguish between *Master/slave* and *Owner/property*. Since only people immersed in this culture would ever be reading this book and be interested in splitting hairs over these words, I'll go into what I think I've learned about the key differences. This doesn't mean you'll agree with me; this is just my opinion.

Ownership doesn't carry an emotional connotation. "Master is owned by the relationship; slave is owned by Master," as Master Dan (Fet = chg2winter) says.

The term "Owner" came into more popular use in about 2007. A few well-respected Masters thought about the contracting phase of M/s and voiced the opinion that a "real slave" would not have the authority to negotiate a contract in the first place. These Masters felt the terms "Owner" and "property" better described the relationship's form. They argued that in lieu of a written contract, a simple exchange of pledges should suffice: the slave would agree to serve and to obey Master/Owner: Master, in turn, would accept complete responsibility for the slave. That would be it. Master now owns this piece of property and its income-producing capacity. The slave has surrendered total personal authority for itself and its assets for total A-Z protection, care, and emotional security.

However… as the M/s community is also populated by lots of smart independent thinkers, some were not quite so fast to go along with this switch in terms. Three groups of challengers emerged.

- One group of questioners felt those promoting the O/p terminology were reaching for political correctness. They felt these people were trying to avoid the words "master" and "slave." There appeared to be no behavior change to accompany the terminology change.
- Another group of questioners pointed out that by describing the relationship as one of "an Owner who has this person as property" seemed to remove either a D/s power exchange or an M/s authority transfer dynamic. O/p seemed to describe the shell of a relationship without describing the driving power within the relationship.
- The third group suggested that (at least in theory), O/p and M/s relationships function differently. In M/s, the slave has quite specifically given authority over itself to another. In O/p an "owner" takes possession of property with no particular thought about how the property feels about it. Think about it: has your car surrendered authority to you? How about the chair you're sitting in?

This third point—that M/s and O/p operate differently—focused on the extent of a Master's authority beyond those an Owner would have. Their argument tended to get expressed like this: "property" is a passive state; "property" might be said to be *along for the ride.*

They do as they are told and use what skills and knowledge they came with. On the other hand, a "slave" is an active position, subject to their Master's decisions about absolutely everything. Thus, while a slave might reasonably expect Master to require them to learn a new language or to go through a voice-training process, or lose 80 pounds, it's not at all clear that "property" would think such requirements are within the *rules of engagement* with their Owner.

By way of summary, while issues of "authority" are handled differently within relationships, I'd argue that unless specifically discussed before their commitment ceremony, an Owner doesn't have the same type of authority over *property* as a Master has over a slave.

Actually, this has been my experience. I was owned for ten years, and I've been fully invested as a slave for two years: these states feel very different. As owned property, I had *much more autonomy.* My time was largely my own, and my Owner permitted me to have other relationships as long as the other people recognized I belonged to her and my primary service was to her. Yes, I was on 24/7 call, but so is your car or camera. As a slave, I am required to be 100% in Master's presence unless at work or running a Master-authorized errand. I make practically no individual decisions. Further, these differences were not a matter of the personalities of my owners; it's a matter of their pre-negotiated expectations.

Subtle role differences between M and s

My friend Sergeant Major (Fet = theSergeantMajor), has come up with a number of brilliant ideas during the years I've known him, and I've included many of my favorites in this book. One such is what he calls: The *order of responsibility* for Masters and slaves. To quote from his article: "The Artistry of Mastery; Picasso or Norman Rockwell." (2014): "I see the role of the master as having a five-part credo; to cherish, respect, protect, lead and guide. Consider those as the five fingers of the hand that the master extends to the slave every day. By extending that hand, the master creates an environment that enables the slave to return the honour with *their own* five-part credo; respect, trust, honour, serve and obey.

The credos are progressive, the acceptance and execution of each action leads to the next; each builds on the one before."

I've created this chart so you can follow the progression more visually.

Order of Master's Responsibilities	Order of slave's Responsibilities
Cherish	Respect
Respect	Trust
Protect	Honor
Lead	Serve
Guide	Obey

I like this approach because it recognizes some of the leader/follower subtleties interlaced throughout this kind of relationship.

Examples of relationship structures

It's difficult to categorize 24/7 M/s structures into "schools of thought" because people run their relationships so differently. At best, by taking a step back and looking for common elements, it's possible to discern certain schools of thought or groups of behavioral characteristics (like the clumps of confetti on the floor I mentioned before).

As I say repeatedly, structured relationships cannot be generalized: what works for one couple has little bearing on what works for another couple. M/s structures thrive with such diversity it's hard to tease out their common characteristics. And, it doesn't help that those of us that live M/s use the same terms while attaching somewhat different meanings to them. For example, "to serve and obey" is a nice broad concept that forms the basis for most—if not all—M/s relationships, but the meanings of "service" and "obedience" are open to wide interpretation.

Moreover, people change over time; you may start an M/s relationship with a clear purpose in mind, but later realize your interest in that purpose has changed. This may not be a big deal, so long as both of you can adapt. However, if your new purpose is radically different from your initial direction, your partner may be unable or unwilling to follow your lead. You'll either have to turn back from your new purpose or change partners in favor of the new purpose. This is an ethical dilemma.

Most relationships begin with lust. Lust has a shelf-life. Sooner or later you'll have to decide whether your next phase is to recommit to having a connected relationship or to escape connection by watching television (or some other activity not involving much contact with your partner).

Here are some characteristics of the better-known M/s models one finds today.

Structure One—Spiritual Model:

- There is high accountability. The way Master treats slave reflects the way Master expects to be treated by those with power over *them*.
- Master is compassionate. Master is concerned about slave's feelings even as slave is required to serve and to obey.
- Total obedience is assumed.
- The couple may live and interact in High Protocol, including slave using third-person speech.
- slave is primarily responsible to serve and to obey: sex may or may not be part of this equation.
- slave is to empty itself of ego to enable Master to lead without resistance.
- They often use *ceremony* to reinforce their bond.
  The slave may be required to have some regular spiritual practice whether or not slave has done so in the past.
- slave is property to be used as Master sees fit.
- The relationship is seen as something like a monastic order: both people are in service to a higher power. Frequently, the service aspect of the relationship is focused on *giving* back to the Community (however, each couple must define "community").

Structure Two—Team Model:
- Master uses the "Leader/manager" model; it's sometimes called the "team model."
- The model is based on compassion, reason, and empathetic guidance.
- Master's view is: "We will do what's good for us" while concurrently recognizing slave as property who ultimately will do as the Team Leader chooses. (The "control model" comes from the viewpoint of: "We will do what's good for Master.")
- This model assumes both members of the relationship are reasonable, intelligent adults who are able to give and understand orders and either can carry them out as given, or ask for clarification. This aspect of the Team Model applies regardless whether you call the structure D/s, or M/s, or anything else.
- The Leader and the manager are on the same team. The Dom/Master/Owner is the team captain.
- The team uses few to no protocols; the slave knows what it needs to do.
- The team is focused on making the relationship more powerful than the separate people.
- This is something like a business model of CEO/COO.

Structure Three—Military Model:
- The Military model is clearly hierarchical at all times.
- slave is expected to be a thinking individual who knows how to approach their superior with ideas and recommendations.
- Master requires a "protocol-heavy" structure: few to no interactions as equals.
- The overall viewpoint is: "We'll be doing this by the book and I wrote the book."
- Master owns slave's time, attention, and future.
- Master often has legal safeguards in place for slave's future.
- Master is focused on ethical and compassionate leadership
- slave's needs come before Master's wants.
- This is something like an 1880s upscale, formal marriage—but with consent.

Structure Four—Control model*:

- Reason, logic, wisdom, and compassion take a back seat to the *might-makes-right* mindset. Master is always right and slave's opinions are largely valueless. Master makes the rules: if slave doesn't like them, slave can leave.
- Master views slave as a living piece of property to be directed as Master sees fit. slave's role is to serve Master's wants; slave is always to be *available*.
- Master's viewpoint is: "We'll be doing what's good for me."
- A slave's value resides in their health and their ability to do what Master asks of them. The slave's value resides in their service (rather than in the person, him/herself).
- slave may not be permitted to bring much or any physical property into the relationship
- Master assumes only as much responsibility for this slave as Master wishes.
- slave has little or no personal autonomy and must be required always to account for its actions, often including going to the bathroom.
- Master tells slave how to dress and the kind of makeup/hair style to wear and how to speak with Master or with others.
- There are consequences for failing to mold itself as Master directs, including dismissal.
- Master will not tolerate much freedom of thought or action: slave is not Master's girlfriend.

* Note about the "Control Model." Raven Kaldera is quick to point out that control models (including the even more severe *adversarial model* that pits Master's wants against the slave's wants) are not inherently bad; they're just not very generalizable. Control models work (to a greater or lesser degree) for those who specifically want to live in a highly controlled structure. Examples include:

- Master may like the idea of having constantly to force the slave to do things. Master may enjoy punishing the slave for failing to do things in a particular way. The slave may seek this structure because they like Master's constant attention and scrutiny. (Without commenting on any possible psychopathology, I've found this model works for couples who are essentially living as adults the way they were treated as children. The slave may be

miserable, but he/she is used to it and can't envision a different way of living.)
- slave may have impulse-control problems and lives comfortably with this Master, who serves as their controller (to keep them in line).
- slave may believe their own creativity and growth benefits from someone totally controlling them. The slave has found a Master who can provide strong and sound guidance and will impose substantial consequences for straying from Master's path.
- slave may so love Master they are willing to commit themselves to Master's service and Master's total direction regardless of any dreams they may have had on their own.

(Those of you who frequent the regional Master/slave conferences can probably put names with these management styles.)

Why do you think I just created that list?

Most relationships are a little of this and a little of that, and at various points throughout this book, you'll hear the "voice" of one or the other of these approaches speaking more loudly than another. In fact, you may be reading in a section largely speaking about one of these types of structures and stumble upon a comment seemingly in almost direct opposition. The "odd" or discordant comment is intended to resonate with the reader who lives in one of the other structure types. I've done this as a reminder: *there is no one right way,* there is only the right way for you.

Leadership style affects relationship structure. Some people lead using the *authority* model; others lead using the *control* model. "Authority-based management" is *outward* looking; "control-based management" is *inward* looking. You either do or do not exhibit the kind of authority that causes your slave to obey. Once your slave recognizes your authority and obeys you, you are free to look beyond the slave to build your world. If your slave does not automatically recognize the scope of your authority, then you must rely on *control* to be sure the slave is doing as you wish. This keeps you looking inward to your slave's behavior. The business parallel is between macromanagement and micromanagement

There are other relationship management issues worth knowing. As an example, consider the "towards vs. away from" personality trait. Some people work *towards* something while other people try to stay *away* from something. Think of an entrepreneurial drive versus the motivations of a CPA or defense attorney. One is pulled *towards* newness and excitement; the other is trained to keep clients *away* from trouble.

It can be useful to understand this *toward/away from* perspective within an M/s relationship to help each partner understand some of the differences/similarities they experience when making important decisions.

M/s relationships as a balancing act

While somewhat different, there are about equal entanglements for a Master as for a slave in most M/s structures. Master's entanglements tend to be financial and practical; slave's entanglements tend to be financial and emotional. Let me explain.

Unless Master earns a substantial salary, they may come to rely upon slave's income to the extent the extra income has increased the Household's living standard. Similarly, to the extent the slave makes Master's life easier, Master may come to rely upon the slave for those domestic and business services. "Payback" ethically requires Master to provide protection and support for the slave's financial, mental, and physical work.

Now, unlike some of the other structures, it is customary/common in M/s relationships for the slave to surrender everything material to Master at the outset. Many slaves are severely limited in what they may bring with them when they move in with a new Master. Also, the slave is expected to choose to support Master's wants and needs over their own wants and, perhaps, over some of their own needs. Yes, Master is expected to act consistently in slave's best interest and to guard/protect slave's particular vulnerabilities, but that's *theory* and when it comes to a particular living couple, personal ethics trump theory. Translation: For the slave more than for the Master, M/s can be a high-risk structure. After all, Master is not likely to have *given up* or *given over* personal wealth/assets to their slave.

This is edgy living. To those looking at us from outside our world, it appears foolhardy. The slave's financial and emotional nakedness can be further distorted by childhood abandonment or rejection fears (particularly as a child of divorced parents). Thus, more than in traditional boyfriend/girlfriend or husband/wife structures, the slave's emotional stability depends upon Master's emotionally-supportive words and deeds.

Comments on some relationship topics

To "own" versus to "possess"

While the concept of "being possessed" is a basic trope among Harlequin Romance novels, there is a big difference between "owning" something and "possessing" something. I'd argue these concepts belong in different logic-sets.

When you own some**thing** you can also be said to possess that *thing*. However, it's not quite as clean-cut when it comes to relationships and the "thing" is a person. I suspect it will help Master to possess the slave's heart to the extent:

- Master is clear that "Master's Path" is also slave's Path—so there is a built-in feedback loop: slave's pleasure comes from pleasing Master and is therefore continually reinforced; and
- Master can demonstrate both accurate and reliable guidance. (*Reliable* only means *consistent: accurate* means *without mistakes.* One can be 100% reliable and consistently miss the target. For an M/s relationship, "accurate guidance" means Master's guidance sings to their particular slave's needs.)

After examining who each of you are as *people*—without the trappings of your relationship structure—it becomes easier to assess your motivations. Your motivations will drive your relationship down one path or another. For example, a couple whose purpose is, "To try to make it through life having some fun while not hurting others" will not be on the path as a couple who has the purpose, "To explore the spiritual dimension of our lives through service to humanity."

However, not everybody spends time thinking about the purpose of their relationship. After all, that's (presumably) one reason you bought this book.

Without a doubt, a couple can live together a long time in some form of quasi-harmony (based on the habits/protocols established after years of living together), but to live in a state where slave feels "possessed" by Master is an entirely different matter. Such a level of connection relies on having absolutely, positively established your reputation for trust, honor, and integrity. These are learned behaviors requiring daily practice. They become routine as you go through the steps preparing for a purposeful life, whether or not for a life of M/s Mastery.

To the extent that Master correctly assesses both slave's needs and dreams, Master (and slave) will have the opportunity to use the M/s dynamic to make magic—whatever their version of *magic* happens to be.

So—with any luck at all, I'm leading you down the path that encourages you to consider your relationship more deeply. Just to start you out with a simple exercise, I'd ask whether the two of you have ever worked through what it is to *be* in a "relationship." As in, what does the word even mean to each of you? I'd certainly encourage you to tackle that one with pen and paper.

Reciprocal service

To come at this topic as objectively as I can (and at the risk of being jarring) I'm going to start with the obedience Masters owe their slaves by leading the relationship by example and with empathy.

Here's what I have come to understand and believe:

> A servant serves Master's needs or is fired;
> a slave serves Master's wants or is released.

> However, Master's wants must not trump slave's needs,
> even when playing by RACK standards.

> slave is in service to Master;
> However, Master is in service to the relationship.

If these ideas also resonate with you as an accurate portrayal of the M/s dynamic, then there is quite a bit of meaning hidden behind these words.

For starters, *in service* in this sense means Master has consciously committed to *right action*. Once on this path, Master's *intent* becomes important. An accidental misstep can still be seen as *right action that failed* in contrast to *wrong action*. For example, it would be wrong for Master to require slave to perform some service that violates the slave's own needs or ethical values. Wrong action may represent a *breach of trust* of the core relationship values. (Just to be clear, the core exchange between Master and slave is this: Master extends total control and protection over slave who pledges to serve and to obey Master.)

This rather heavy/serious line of thought brings up an issue concerning one's capacity to Master: can Master exert total authority and control over another person without abusing their trust? Said casually, "Does Master have the emotional intelligence to watch the rain without being pulled into the storm? Can Master remain calm when Drama comes to pay you a visit?" (Note: In Chapter 4 when I discuss *leadership* I'll spend some time discussing how to *have an upset* rather than *being upset*. For now, I'll leave you with the question: "Does this person have enough emotional control to be able to lead this structured relationship responsibly?")

So, where are we? We have a Master who is serving the relationship by endeavoring to act ethically and reliably with respect to the slave in their service. The question now becomes: "What does all this mean in terms of giving orders to slave?"

For an order to be in the slave's best interest, Master and slave must be in *alignment*. Alignment can be a tricky thing. You may be in alignment one moment and out-of-alignment in another moment. Said differently, Master may wish slave to do "X" and, for whatever reason, slave feels doing "X" would not be a *gift* but an *obligation* to Master based upon being the slave.

Now: in most instances, the slave would realize, "liking it has nothing to do with it" and would follow the order. However, in a few situations, the order may place Master and slave at severe odds. For example, Master may decide their slave must limit or totally stop contact with someone, perhaps a family member. Even though the order may be extremely uncomfortable for both people, it is understandable as long as Master believes it is in the long-term best interest of the slave and/or the relationship. On the other hand, to the extent Master's order traumatizes the slave and is **not** intended to benefit the slave or the relationship, it may be an unethical order. The litmus test is whether or not Master would object to the order if the roles were reversed. If yes, the order may actually be an ethical breach representing an abuse of Master's power over their slave—and a devastating breach of trust from the slave's perspective.

Along similar lines, while Master expects (or requires or demands) obedience from the slave, does Master model the desired behavior? Does Master model ethical work/business practices? Does Master model good eating and exercise habits? Does Master drive the speed limit? Master must model the behavior they seek from slave, yes?

Realistically, Master is probably seeking a slave whose *intent* is to fulfill the spirit of Master's wishes regardless of the specifics. Strict obedience to Master's requests is probably less critical than the intent underlying slave's actions. This is a touchy point, as some Masters may become upset to the point of punishing slave for failure to follow directives in a specific way, while—in fact—slave has completely fulfilled the spirit of the directive. This ties back to a comment a few paragraphs earlier about Master having the emotional control to lead the relationship: Master may need objectivity to discern slave's intentions before reacting to a task completed differently than Master had expected.

So: what *does* Master want from slave? While there are lots of potential answers, here are a few generalizations:
- Master wants slave to listen to an order and then repeat it to Master to confirm slave's understanding is aligned with Master's intent.
- Master wants slave to understand the general gist of an order efficiently/effectively without troubling Master with the details.

- Master may want slave to do exactly what is ordered without interjecting anything of slave's own viewpoint.

This last approach can have unintended consequences for Master, because the slave may feel their opinions/experiences are being ignored and disrespected. If this is the case…

- Master and slave may be out of sync: as Master Michael points out, relationships have ebb and flow cycles—the couple may temporarily be out of alignment.
- Master and this slave have different models of how an M/s structure should be run: they may have a fundamental disagreement over their respective roles in their structure.
- Master may be personally insecure and has entered the M/s life in order to disguise such insecurities by giving orders that are not to be questioned.
- Etc.

Obviously, some orders will be completed more successfully than others. Some orders may not be completed as Master wished or intended. Again, we're at philosophical crossroads. Masters interpret "communication failure" in different ways.

- Some will project their personal demons onto the other person and react to those as though the slave was willfully disobedient (we'll cover this later).
- Some will suspect their slave is demonstrating resistance to their authority (an indication the entire relationship is unstable).
- Some will realize (or suspect) their own order was either imprecise or incomplete and that the slave acted in good faith but didn't achieve the results Master sought or expected (at issue: "Did you hear what I wanted you to hear?").
- Some realize everything happens is an opportunity to go to the next opportunity.

Attitude is everything as the saying goes.

There is a great lesson some of us learn in the M/s culture: when Master interprets slave as doing something "wrong" it brings friction and upset into the relationship. What the slave did isn't actually *wrong*, it's just what the slave did, given slave's particular background, training, and "brain wiring." The challenge is to figure out how make the reality of what slave did fit in with the reality of your relationship. If you cast slave's action as "wrong," then you may be missing the reality that the slave's entire service to you is a gift from his/her heart.

Remember: slave's greatest fear is in not pleasing Master. This, then, brings us to the distinction between can't vs. won't. As Raven Kaldera mentioned one time in a workshop, "The *can'ts* are Master's obligation; the *wont's* are slave's obligation." He goes on to say: "Just because there is a 'can't' in your slave doesn't mean that you should throw out the slave; it only means that you need to use the slave differently."

This line of thought can be summarized this way: Master's orders may legitimately test slave's willingness, but should not be used to test the slave's abilities. When orders are used to test a slave's abilities, the situation comes close to being a setup for failure. Once the slave feels Master is setting it up for failure, other (dark) doubts begin to rattle around in the slave's head. Master won't want to encourage dark doubts.

Which brings us full circle: while slave is in service to Master, Master is in service to the relationship. Master has a lot of juggling to do.

Are you at the *cause* or *effect* of yourself?

Here's another exercise I'd encourage you to tackle (with or without your partner). Try to figure out the degree to which you are in command of yourself. Try to assess the extent your reactions to people and life are really under your own control. I mention this because most reactions are nearly automatic and largely controlled by the way the person was brought up, combined with culture-bound assumptions and preferences.

Anyway, let me start you out with some personal philosophy (well… *assertions*, really)…

Everyone is doing the best they can with what they know. While it is generally true that people are doing the best they can with what they know, people really don't know very much. This is compounded, because people don't know what they don't know, so they *think* they know enough to be just fine. They're wrong, which is why people have so much trouble doing well in life. Translation: relationships (*lives*, really) are often less than their potential because the partners don't have the skills, tools, or perspective to alter their course. Partly, this occurs because not many people think about radically altering their usual way of being in the world. However, this state remains fixed in place because when they *do* broach the subject in their minds, the amount of work involved in making such dramatic personal change is simply overwhelming. So, they stop thinking about it.

You already have whatever you're looking for. This is a double-edged sword, for while this may be true, you may not be happy about what you have. If you have ended up with something you don't believe you were looking for, it's up to you to refine/redefine what you're looking for. This may involve redefining your vision of yourself and learning skills and behaviors that would ultimately create a different reality than you currently have. Translation: only you are responsible for what you are learning and how you are acting. If you don't like the result of your current approach to life, change your approach.

Taken together, these two points mean this: *You happen to life, life does not happen to you, and it's your move.*

Even though relationships all have subtle differences, those who walk the M/s path have an unusual opportunity. Those on this path have the opportunity to grow not just in self-understanding but also in their understanding how to create a symbiotic relationship. A symbiotic relationship means the whole is greater (stronger, smarter) than the separate individuals. But, you have to choose it and act upon that choice. Choose and act. A dream fulfilled is a choice acted upon. Of course, everyone who has ever had to make a decision realizes *not to act* is also a choice and a decision.

So: this is a book about choices. I'll be throwing all kinds of ideas/concepts at you and you get to choose which are nutty and which might make some sense.

Master's versus slave's motivations

Power and control

There are a few conference presenters whom I go out of my way to see. These are the people who toss powerful ideas into the room as if to see who might be awake enough to catch them. Master Skip Chasey is one of those presenters. I was busily typing away in his class on "Unfettered Restraint" at the 2014 Master/slave Conference when he came out with two stunning sentences:

- "Because of the D/s authority and control imbalance, the D-type has all the power and control."
- "Because Master's authority over the slave depends totally on slave granting Master such authority, slave has most control."

Wow! What insight. I've read those lines over and over and they remain the stunning insight they started out to be.

Once said out loud, it makes perfect sense. Also, it leads to other ideas, such as differences in motivations between a Master and a slave.

Motivations

Motivations differ at many levels. For example, the *kind* of M/s structure in which you've cloaked yourself is driven by your combined motivations to "be" a certain way as a couple. You may want to look formal to outsiders and maintain a high-protocol private life, or you may not care how others think of you, and you're following a spiritually-based inner relationship. There are infinite combinations. Bear in mind: the motivations that bind the two of you together is one thing, your separate motivations are a different thing. Here are a few ideas about motivations to start you thinking about motivations within your own relationship.

Typical slave motivations:
- to feel the communication channel is completely open and honest (sometimes called *transparency*);
- to feel connected (perhaps that your protocols are designed to maintain relationship connection or that you have mutual projects);

- to feel emotionally safe and secure; and
- to know Master is still leading the relationship ethically, and that Mater's leadership makes sense.

Typical Master motivations:
- to feel their authority is recognized;
- to know the slave is working as hard as possible within their knowledge and skill sets;
- to know the slave is remaining true to their path ("path" must be described/defined);
- to know slave's protocols also feed Master's sense of *pride in ownership;* and
- to know the slave will follow Master's directives.

Love in service-based relationships

I'm not speaking about the emotion called "love" in this section; I'm speaking about how the concept called "love" fits into Master's leadership style. To repeat a concept initially articulated by Master Skip Chasey (and picked up by Jack Rinella in his marvelous book: *Partners in Power*), Masters often feel: *If my needs are being met, it must be love. So, I'll say that I love you so you'll continue to meet my needs.*

We've all heard terms such as *Masters' love* and *slaves' love.* The expanded explanation of these phrases is: "While Master often *loves* slave, slave more often is *in love* with Master."

First, some opening quips:
- M/s relationships tend to rely on *authority;* D/s relationships tend to rely on *power.*
- There is love and there is fear: when you love you needn't fear, when you fear you cannot love. While this sounds good in theory, the fear of abandonment can cause someone to proclaim their love even more strongly. This is particularly true among people with low self-esteem and low feelings of self-worth. They proclaim their love often, hoping for reciprocal confirmation from their partner—to help keep their panic down.

Chapter 1: Relationships

- Love doesn't *necessarily* conflict with slavery; it's really an issue of how you *name* what's important. It's how you channel your energy.

In a general way, M/s relationships diverge over the *love* issue. While some M/s couples maintain a love-based relationship, others maintain a service-based relationship. They don't always mix.

We've all known love is complicated since our teenage years. By itself, *love* is a complex state, but it's much more complicated when it's combined with an *authority-imbalanced service-based* relationship. So… writing about something as personal as *love* combined with the variety of ways Masters define *service* makes it challenging to say something here that will touch you, especially when you've been doing this for a while and believe you have what you want.

Actually, the topic is made even more complex because some see M/s as a spiritual calling and others are trying to model the structure on traditional slavery. Somewhere towards the middle, you have those who belong to the camp of what we might call "authority-based enlightened leadership."

So, merely by way of thinking about love in service-based relationships, let me try to separate some of the basic motivations. Remember: I'm not writing to change your minds or behaviors, only to help make some of the options stand out in ways that may not yet have occurred to you.

As much as it's complicated, the Master/slave community has some rather distinct "camps" when it comes to this topic. I'm going to write this section as though these are hard-and-fast and well-defined statements: they are not. I'm simply trying to draw distinctions between these viewpoints. By the way—I've collected these ideas from many sources, so some of the bullet-points are harder or softer than others.

Love as central to the relationship: Without love, why bother? Some M/s couples (particularly those who are married) seem to compartmentalize their emotions based on the context of the interaction. For example, Master may establish protocols to bring the slave into mindful presence if Master suspects slave is *drifting* into a vanilla-like response pattern. However, this does not address *Master* also drifting back to Vanillaville.

Master *in love* with slave degrades the structure: Master compromises authority and control by being in love. "Love" is one thing, but "in love" is quite another thing. An "in love" state compromises Master's focus, authority, and control. Emotions and emotional connection compromise the intent of the relationship. Master can't be sure whether slave is obeying out of love or out of obedience. Master's **objectivity** is compromised once they *need something* from the slave—such as love. Master's **control** is compromised once they compromise their wants. When Master adopts the viewpoint they must "give a little to get a little," the death knell is sounded.

slave being *in love* contaminates *obedience*: SlaveMaster and others believe love ruins obedience. They believe that doing things for love is not always "doing what is right" for the relationship. From SlaveMaster's point of view, our duty in life is to find our inner authentic voice and obey it. "Falling in love" can interfere with doing this. He would argue—as I do in this section—that there's a distinction between "in love" and "love." Being "in love" means that the person is mostly focused on Eros (see diagram, below). Representing SlaveMaster, slave 7 expanded, noting, "*Obedience* comes first, and *love* naturally follows but if love is put first, obedience does **not** naturally follow."

This "love" discussion it's irrelevant: M/s is a relationship structure based on *service and obedience*. Love is a different discussion. In the Military, the lieutenant doesn't have to "love" the Major to follow orders.

M/s is a *calling; love* may or may not have anything to do with it: Master/slave is a gift the Universe has given you; your task on Earth is to work with that gift. Every negative has a positive: work with the positives and ignore the negatives. Your only reward for focusing on negatives is to draw them to you. Focus locks things into place, whether those are positive things or negative things. You can be

Chapter 1: Relationships

called only to a small portion of a person and may not much care for some of Master/slave's other parts.

Okay, I'll stop and move on.

One way of thinking about all this *lust/friendship/calling* material is to go back to the terminology developed by Greek philosophers during Aristotle's time. Three of the four aspects are:

- Agape is love in a *spiritual* sense and refers to unconditional love based on *choice*.
- Eros is *romantic love*. This is physical, passionate love with sensual desire and longing. *Eros* is pure emotion without the balance of logic.
- Phila is *affectionate regard* or *friendship*. This form of love includes loyalty to friends, family, and community, and requires virtue, equality and familiarity.

Storge, a fourth aspect of love according to the Greek philosophers, refers to the kind of affection felt by parents for offspring. For the purposes of illustrating my point, I'd like to leave *storge* aside and concentrate on *Eros, phila,* and *agape*.

This material is relevant, because those in relationships may not feel pulled towards the same kind of love as their partners. Differences can lead to hurt feelings. Some would describe their feelings for their partner as a combination of *Eros* and *agape,* while others might describe it closer to a combination of *phila* and *Eros* with some *agape* thrown in. Obviously, this is another area where couples can benefit from thinking about and discussing the kind of love they feel towards one another (and the purpose of their relationship).

Master Michael pointed out that Guy Baldwin, when discussing "love" in *Ties that Bind,* shared the phrase: "I love you 'cause you know me, I trust you with my Self." Master Michael added that: "I love that quote because it really fits where I think love goes in an M/s relationship and can encompass whether it is Eros, Agape and/or Phila."

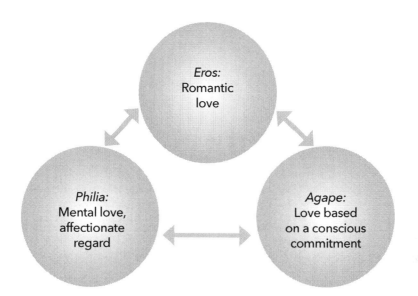

Permit me to make a few additional comments. It can be risky to wallow in *Eros* love—even though it's a lot of fun and feels good. *Eros* is usually thought of as fleeting. In modern English, *Eros* is really a euphemism for the kind of emotions referred to as *new relationship energy*. Conventional wisdom says emotional connection at this level lasts about three months. Jay Wiseman refers to this period as *The Three-Month Crazies.* Those who require *Eros* to feel comfortable in a relationship purposefully and slowly dole out new experiences in an effort to extend the *Three Month Crazies* and ride the NRE wave as long as possible.

Obviously, stable relationships depend both on liking and loving your partner. *Philia* means loving friendship. People who think about such topics assert that by first developing *philia* and then blending it with *Eros*, a couple can more naturally meet their partner's needs while concurrently fulfilling their own.

This model is threatened by violating the bonds either of love or of friendship. In fact, because *philia* is *close loving friendship,* breaking trust at this level (through dishonesty, poor integrity, or disloyalty) usually also breaks the tie with romantic love. This occurs because violating the trust of friendship by someone who supposedly loves you can become an unforgivable hurt.

Agape describes one's love of the spirit within another person or, more broadly, within God. *Agape* is reached through the intellect: one evaluates a person or concept and makes a choice to love them/it. "*Agape* is the perfect love that originates from God and is the characteristic of God." (Raven Kaldera)

Many couples living successfully in an M/s relationship have learned how to thrive in the area between *Eros* and *agape.* They have learned how to combine the emotional impact/feelings of *Eros* and apply them to a teacher/guru/sensei archetype. When you hear people repeat Master Skip Chasey's observation, "D/s is about the mental body, M/s is about the spiritual body" this is what they mean.

I'm spending time describing *love* in this detail because it may help you to more effectively communicate your wants and needs for each other (and for the relationship) once you can clarify how you feel about one another.

Happiness

Here's a tidbit of information I found years ago and worked into my M/s life. In short, it's a principle from psychology referred to as *hedonic adaptation* (also called *the hedonic treadmill theory*). This theory describes the tendency of humans to return quickly to a relatively stable level of happiness despite major positive or negative events or life changes. According to this theory, as a person makes more money, expectations and desires rise in tandem—and as a consequence, there is in no permanent gain in happiness. This theory compares the pursuit of happiness to a person on a treadmill who has to keep working just to stay in the same place.

I'm bringing this up because the Hedonic (or Happiness) Set Point has gained interest throughout the field of positive psychology where it has been further developed and revised. The theory helps us to understand happiness as both an individual and a societal goal. Concerning our

M/s lives, the theory is important because you can learn how to use *purposefulness* and *intention* to avoid changing your emotional set-point. Once your set-point is stable, you and your slave will be able to remain happy and satisfied with what you share together. Personally, I've come to rely upon two techniques to anchor purposefulness and intention. First, create protocols that constantly affirm your unusual structure (speech, stance, interaction protocols); and second, learn how better to manage your "learner/judger" decision-making process.

(Note: In *Change Your Questions, Change Your Life*, Marilee Adams has a "Choice Map." That map shows how the blame-focused Judger path relies on automatic reactions and sets up win-lose situations while the more thoughtful Learner path is solution-focused and sets up win-win situations. If this topic seems interesting to you, I'd encourage you to look it up. Bread crumbs…)

Chapter 2: Mastery

Mastery can be a tricky subject. It can be tricky for all kinds of reasons, but perhaps most obviously, there are no *standards* for personal mastery so you don't really know (objectively) when you get there. One person's Master is another person's dilettante.

Lolly Daskal, a contributor to the website www.Quoa.com, has come up with a definition I like, even though it is not quantifiable: "Personal mastery is the discipline of formulating our dreams, hopes and desires. It is cultivation between tension, vision and reality."

Personally, I've not found it necessary to quantify a concept such as mastery. I recognize a master when I meet one. In the more general sense, *mastery* is one's personal assessment that someone has attained expert skills or knowledge in their chosen field. When one gets to this level, others recognize you for what you are.

Master's Statement of Mastery

This is who I am;
this is what I value;
this is what I will and will not do;
this is how I choose to act.

Chapter 2: Mastery

This section is devoted to teasing out components of mastery in an effort to help you assess not only where you stand on this Path, but also to give you ideas about other places you may wish to look for more information on the subject.

Mastery takes work, regardless of the area of study. People generally prefer to *get by* rather than to study and work. There are many areas where you would *think* people would be highly motivated to study to become really good, but they don't. *Sex techniques, parenting, leadership skills,* and *communication* come immediately to mind. Have you ever taken a course in *how to give great sexual experiences* or in *how to communicate effectively with respect and power?* Probably not. Even so, you think you're good at sex, and that you're a persuasive communicator. Why do you think that? What evidence do you have?

Other than in a work environment, I don't have the sense that our culture supports *thinking.* Ours is a consumer-based hedonistic culture that supports simple-minded television programming, blood-and-guts movies, and watching lots and lots of sports. Do you know many people who belong to a book club? How about a discussion group (excluding your local MAsT chapter, please)?

So: how does one make time to become a Master of something while submerged in a majority culture encouraging mediocrity over meritocracy? Hmmmm. Blow up your TV? Move to the country? Simplify your life?

But, you're certainly very special to be reading this book. This is a thinking book hiding in a culture that itself is so unusual there aren't likely to be more than a few thousand couples worldwide living this way. This means that you're open to ideas. This is a good thing.

In my experience, people who have grown and matured over time are first and foremost in control of themselves. They are disciplined: they keep their word. You can count on them. At some point, they made a conscious decision to become a master of their monkey brain, their reactive self. This certainly takes thoughtful effort, for one cannot do *mastery* casually.

This is a good place to refocus on Masters in the context of Master's role in an M/s relationship.

By assuming the mantle of *Master* you are assuming responsibility for managing yourself while concurrently

> If people only knew how hard I work to gain my mastery, it wouldn't seem so wonderful at all.
>
> —Michelangelo Buonarroti
> Italian architect, painter, &
> sculptor (1475—1564)

serving as trainer, mentor, and guide. Managing another person successfully is as much art as science; it is a process that requires as much finesse as it requires mastery of new skills and knowledge. As my friend Brett (Fet = LTD) says: "Master is an artist whose medium is person who—for lack of a better word—is called a *slave.*"

The Rules of Mastery

I know, the title of this section has made the hairs stand up on your scalp. Not a problem: I'm not the one proposing the rules—I know better. However, mastery is mastery and the rules I'm reprinting here have to do with *mastery* as a transferrable skill. Change "bonsai" to "slave" and you have a pretty compelling guide to Mastery in the sense that we mean it. Thanks to Master Stephen (Stephen_Mar on Fet) for using this story in one of his presentations on Master/slave relations. Thanks VERY much to its author for permitting me to reprint it in this book. This lesson is an allegory of Master/slave management.

The Bonsai Master
Copyright © 1993 by Horace A. Vallas, Jr. (www.hav.com/bonsai.html)

It takes years of patience and attention to develop a fine bonsai. It takes at least as long to become a master practitioner. There is no such thing as an "instant bonsai"— nor a "one-minute master."

Chapter 2: Mastery

A skilled and practiced eye is required to recognize promising bonsai material—backing-off or squinting in order to obtain proper perspective. One must learn to identify the fundamental structure and form of a potential bonsai, selectively ignoring tangle or sparseness. Order can be brought to tangle—and sparseness can be used to advantage—but the tree itself will dictate its optimum style.

The master uses rules of style as guidelines only. He knows that rigid adherence often leads to disappointing results. A master directs his efforts toward enhancing—not fighting—a tree's natural tendencies.

Training is a process of refinement. First consideration is given to the trunk. It may take several years to obtain an appropriate taper. Next, the main branches are refined to provide the general shape of the canopy. This too may require several growing seasons to accomplish. Finally, the branchlets are tended and the bonsai is fully revealed.

The master gives as much—or even more—attention to the back of a tree as he does to its front. He knows that it is the back that provides the depth required for a dramatic frontal view.

Throughout training, the roots of the tree are cared for. Root mass is reduced slowly, over time. Large roots in particular must be removed gradually, in stages, to allow new feeder roots to form and take over supply needs.

During training, wire and other appliances are used sparingly and as unobtrusively as possible, allowing for pleasant viewing even while the tree is being trained. Appliances are left in place only long enough to accomplish their purpose and are removed before scaring or other damage occurs.

Shaping takes place in stages with consideration given to the maturity of the tree. A young tree or branch has the suppleness of youth. More patience is required to bend a mature branch.

If one is too aggressive, an important branch can be damaged or lost causing general loss of balance or form.

The nature of the tree will dictate its needs in terms of environment and nutrition. The master knows that the pine likes good drainage provided by sand but the bald-cypress will flourish in bog. He knows that a quince can stand freezing temperatures that would kill a black-olive. A feeding schedule is designed for each tree individually. The master knows the reward for such individual attention.

The master is skilled in the use of controlled stress as part of training. He knows when to withhold water. He knows when root pruning will lead to leaf-size reduction. He knows when to withhold feeding to enhance flowering. The master knows how much stress his tree can stand, and when and how to remove stress when its work is done.

In selecting the component pieces of a forest planting, the master again uses nature as a guide. The role, scale, placement and species of each tree is carefully planned and executed. The result is a harmonious and accurate reflection of a natural forest with its dark places, sunny meadows, shaded glens and root-broken paths.

The master is careful in selection of the pot that will serve as home for his bonsai. The pot must enhance the beauty of the tree's form and coordinate with its size. It should provide correct contrast to the tree's color, blending subtly with the tree to form a pleasing whole.

Pruning is performed throughout a bonsai's lifetime, but only as necessary to maintain proper form. Balance is maintained between root and canopy, and trunk and branch. Pruning is performed in a manner that strengthens the tree. The master knows that pruning too much or too often can weaken or even kill a tree.

At times it is beneficial to allow periods of wild, unrestrained growth. Wild branches are often left in place for several seasons to strengthen and thicken the trunk. Later, these can be removed and rooted to form new trees. Many fine bonsai began life as cuttings.

Training of a bonsai is never really finished for it is a living and ever changing thing. Over the years, with practiced observation and close attention, the master learns the nature and the cycles of his trees. He knows their seasons. He knows their spring and fall colors. He knows their summer canopies and their winter forms. He knows when branch and bud swell will occur. He knows how much mid-summer heat and sun can be tolerated. He knows when each is flourishing and when one is suffering.

A master is tireless in his attention. He can be found daily, out among his trees, both reveling in—and wondering at—their ability to reflect the majesty, strength, and mystery of creation. The master is ever grateful for his chance to participate.

Should a fine old bonsai reach the end of its life, the master will show his concern to the end. No trash heap awaits a favored companion.

And finally, when the master reaches the end of his season, he will pass his charges on to another...perhaps student...perhaps teacher...with knowledge that his care will continue through other hands.

Great allegory: profoundly appropriate, in my opinion.

Working on your personal Mastery

If I were writing a simple relationships book, this is where I'd say something like this: Experience teaches us how stable long-lasting relationships succeed to a greater or lesser degree based on each partner's:

- beliefs about their self-worth;
- abilities to separate needs from wants;
- level of empathy, common sense, and insightfulness;
- degree of contentment with their personal lives;
- ability to manage time and money;
- condition of their mental and physical wellbeing; and
- other such generalities.

Just as there are different ways to successfully lead another person, there are also many ways of learning things in life. Later in this book, I'll go into more depth about leading skills and learning skills; I'm side-stepping them right now because I'd like to bring up some points bearing directly on honing your own mastery. As usual, some of these will be relevant to you and others won't.

In my experience, when it comes to Mastering someone, it helps if you have some overall idea about your personal vision. My friend H0und (Fet name) expressed this most clearly in a conversation about

> Although you have responsibility for anything over which you have authority, you can only control two things: your thoughts and your actions. That makes *Mastering someone* quite a personal challenge.

successfully leading an M/s relationship when he said: "I visualize my own goals while listening to her goals." Very insightful; but I think much of what H0und says is insightful.

This leads us to a truism: If you're in a leadership role and you don't know your own strengths and weaknesses, you're going to have a tough time giving competent orders: it's a case of the blind leading the blind, as it were.

Worse, people often have a distorted sense of how good they are at things, sex, relationships, and leadership being three examples of topics ripe for self-delusion. These are examples of areas where people tend to rely on their (often imagined) past successes to

Chapter 2: Mastery

excuse a lack of focus and attention on their present situation. That won't work. As some pundit once quipped: Forget the past. No one becomes successful in the past.

Which brings up the question: how well do you know yourself? Historically, how have you managed yourself in crises? Were you proud of how you behaved? Did others around you think to themselves how mature and dynamic you were? Did you stand up for what was right?

Some of these questions are personally embarrassing to answer honestly. People frequently go through life trying to avoid responsibility for their role. Many people want to do something magical versus doing magical things as a matter of routine. Think of it this way: most of us think of ourselves as someone who—just at the right moment—will dash into a burning house to rescue someone and get a lot of attention. But there aren't a lot of burning houses around, so we lack practice. As a result, when a burning building shows up, we panic and call the fire department. They're the people responsible for dashing into burning houses to rescue people. Not our job. Above our pay grade.

Now how about our role in our own relationships: we're the General. It IS our responsibility to master leadership and communication skills and such. Moment by moment, we are expected to take responsibility for giving orders as much as the slave is expected to take responsibility for obeying orders. We are expected to be constantly mindful of our personal responsibility for another. But, sometimes things get in the way. Sometimes, Masters are just people.

In my experience, three areas stand out for having the potential to bring one out of their "personal mastery" head space. I'd like to introduce them to you here, as they are part of the foundation of understanding about this topic. We'll run into them in greater detail later in the book.

The need to be right. The need to be right shuts people off from hearing a different viewpoint. This is a variant of the usually-male mental affliction that leads them to believe that they can solve any problem by using a bigger hammer. This "closed-down-charging-forward" approach to relationship upsets actually has some pretty well-hidden roots. Just to start you down an interesting pathway, you might consider picking up a copy of a marvelous little book containing one of the keys to gaining new perspectives. It's called, *The Usual Error* (by Pace and Kyeli Smith) and it describes the many benefits that come from not assuming that other people are just like you.

Careless word use. Careless word use communicates lack of attention (or caring) to your listener. Careless word use encompasses nondescript filler words such as "things" or "stuff" or "whatever" rather than fully-fleshed phrases. Careless word use can also involve employing such vanilla terms such as "thank you" and "I love you" rather than terms specifically tailored to your M/s structure, such as "thank you slave" or "boy/girl, Master loves you." In this last example, the very familiarity of these overused phrases simply fails to register at all on the intended beneficiary. Silence would probably be equally effective, for you say and hear "thank you" and "I love you" so frequently and casually that these phrases are all but meaningless in an M/s setting.

Decision exhaustion. Master simply gets worn out by having to make all the decisions. Later, when I bring this topic up again, I'll propose some protocols you can consider for avoiding this particular rut.

Mastery as a concept

Malcolm Gladwell, the amazing author of *Blink, The Tipping Point, What the Dog Saw, David and Goliath,* and *Outliers,* says that to become very good at something you have to have logged over 5,000 hours of active practice; to become an expert at something, you have to have spent over 10,000 hours of active practice. Ten thousand hours. Let's take a look at that for a minute.

However you cut it, 10,000 hours is a long time. In absolute terms, there are 8,760 hours in a year, so 10,000 hours is about 417 days, or about a year and two months. Calculating with further discernment, 10,000 hours is 1,250 eight-hour workdays, which (when divided into 5-day work weeks) reveals 10,000 hours to be about 250 work weeks: roughly 5 years. And remember, that's five years of eight-hour days of focused practice. None of us are practicing M/s leadership eight hours a day, five days a week.

Chapter 2: Mastery

Let's dice this again. I suspect the most time that you or I can actually "do" M/s is four hours a night (presuming you do NOT have a television), seven nights a week, plus 10 hours combined on weekend days. That feel about right? Bad news: you won't quite get to 2,000 hours in a year. And, if you have a TV, you can write that one right off. You're not practicing M/s if you're watching TV. Although you may be together physically, you're certainly not together psychologically. No, we don't have a TV. Wouldn't allow one in the house. Never have.

What's the take-away? Any way you look at it, anything close to 10,000 hours is a huge time commitment and explains why real masters (of any discipline) are so rare.

But, you can get pretty good at it, and this book is aimed at helping you get even better by focusing your areas of potential study.

The way I've come to look at it, there are three stages of Mastery: being, knowing, doing. This section offers a variety of perspectives/resources about how, exactly, one can prepare for or perfect one's Mastery.

- "Master what is yours to master; master your reactions to the world around you—how you drive, how you relate to others, how you process information, etc.," says Master Stephen (Stephen_Mar on Fet). He adds: "Put as much effort into the boring as you put into what is interesting."
- "Master must master three energies and bring them to bear within their relationship. These are playfulness (injecting humor, the creative spark), vulnerability (openness and sensitivity) and fierceness (strength, standing your ground, conviction)" says my friend Senor Jaime (Fet=SenorJaime). Well done, Senor Jaime.
- *"Willpower is like a muscle*, it can be fatigued with use" concludes Roy Baumeister (author of *Willpower: Rediscovering the Greatest Human Strength*). While *willpower* cannot perform indefinitely, the more you use it the more it is available for you to use. He says that while at first you'll run out of willpower even to build your mental muscle, you can, with focus and application, build up quite a capacity to exert your will at will. Willpower is generic, according to Baumeister: the focus of your willpower doesn't matter. I think the summary expression is: "Just do it!"

This, according to the way my Asperger mind works, is just the place to insert a note about *mindfulness.* (Remember my point of view: you're in an M/s relationship in order to do something very different with your life than you would if you were in an unstructured relationship. With that, I offer you some resources on being present with your partner.)

Like building willpower, it's easier to speak about establishing mindful practices than to do them. *Mindfulness* calls for you to realize that whatever happened a few seconds/hours/days/years ago are fixed in stone. You can't do anything about the past, and what you are doing right now, this moment, influences your next minute/hour/day/year/life. Mindfulness involves letting go of *what was* and embracing *what is.* It also means you will have to stop dreaming of *what may be* unless *what you are doing right now* is part of the process that can make your dream become real. Mindfulness is a bedfellow of twins: *focus* and *intent.* I have four really great references if you want to join me on this path. Honestly, you'll probably be interested in all four; they're very different.

- *How to Train a Wild Elephant: And Other Adventures in Mindfulness* by Jan Cozen Bays. (The book provides a 52 week-long practices to help us cultivate mindfulness as we go about our ordinary, daily lives. She presents each exercise with tips on how to remind yourself to stay mindful, and a short life-lesson connected with it. The author is a physician and Zen master.)
- *Focusing* by Eugene Gendlin (The book consists of six easy-to-master steps that identify the way thoughts and emotions are held within the body. This knowledge helps you to make personal change. The book is based on groundbreaking research conducted at the University of Chicago.)
- *The Practicing Mind* by Thomas Sterner (By teaching you how to love the process of learning, the book demonstrates how to learn skills for any aspect of life, from golfing to business to parenting. It focuses on the often-overlooked science and art of *practice*. This is vital material for trainers.)
- *The Miracle of Mindfulness* by Thich Nhat Hanh. (The book offers gentle anecdotes and practical exercise as a means of learning the skills of mindfulness--being awake and fully aware. Master Michael suggests this book and adds: "Although Buddhist in nature, it is an excellent book on mindfulness.")

Chapter 2: Mastery

I'll leave this section with a couple of concepts for you to consider: I don't have the space in this book to expand on these ideas—that's your task if you like them.

- In the minute, you can find the infinite.
- Masters can't command happiness but they can create an environment of lightness and joy.

Learning stages

I spent time in the companion book (*Master/slave Mastery: Updated handbook of concepts, approaches, and practices*) describing visible and invisible knowledge and the four stages of learning (unconscious incompetence, conscious incompetence, conscious competence, and unconscious competence). I don't want to repeat the same material here. However, I'd like to point out that the consequence of *unconscious incompetence* is referred to as "the arrogance of youth." This is the stage during which a person thinks they know everything they need to know—particularly about pragmatic things such as doing the dishes, sweeping the floor, or fucking. In fact, they seldom know enough to know they don't know enough.

As this relates to Mastery, many people who have a dominant personality (or perhaps who have managed to raise a family) believe that they know how to be a leader. Right. With very few exceptions, this is pure unconscious incompetence. Every leader I've ever met was dripping with knowledge about leadership theory and practice. I've listed some resources in the Supplements.

Are all Masters dominants?

It depends: how do you define "Master" and "Dominant." After all, if you consider anybody who owns a slave to be a Master, then—by the very nature of probabilities and bell-curve distributions—you're bound to come up with some Masters who don't appear very dominant to other Masters.

On the other hand, someone who falls at the lower end of the "dominant-submissive" scale may end up with a slave who is willing to serve them because of who they are, irrespective of the amount of "dominance" they exhibit.

Conclusion: the question is irrelevant. If you are responsible for a slave, you're a Master and are responsible for learning how to behave like one.

Mastering emotional reactions

This is a touchy subject: it is a difficult, slippery, and multi-layered subject.

But, we have to go there. You can't live in an "edgy" relationship structure without having an emotional train-wreck or two. In my own current relationship, Jen refers to our "touchy subjects" as the elephant in the room. One or the other of us gets reactive when certain subjects come up so we pull back, realizing it's not yet the right time to engage them; emotions are still too raw.

However, not everyone would shrink back from confronting the elephants. For example, Raven Kaldera says: "If Master is afraid to engage in a discussion with slave because Master fears slave's emotions, then it's those emotions that run the relationship, not Master. Master must feel free to speak without concern over what the other person may think or how they react."

A decision to "engage the elephant" presumes Master is a skilled communicator and knows quite a bit about managing uncomfortable conversations. Also, it presumes Master is engaging in the emotion-laden conversation in a way they believe can be successful with Master's particular slave **and** the conversation is both necessary and serves the Relationship. There are a lot of qualifiers in those two sentences.

If you'd like some help in these areas, here are some resources:
- *Crucial Conversations Tools for Talking When Stakes Are High, Second Edition* by Kerry Patterson, Joseph Grenny, Ron McMillan, and Al Switzler. This million-seller book can help to prepare for high-stakes conversations, to transform your anger and hurt feelings into words and dialogue, to make it safe to talk about almost anything, and to be persuasive rather than abrasive.
- *Self-Discipline and Emotional Control* by Tom Miller (an audio CD). This is a very in-your-face confrontational training course; it's not for the faint of heart. On the other hand, this style is

probably necessary to wake you up to the battle between your horse and your rider (your "monkey brain" versus your "rational brain"). I've recommended this course many times, for in my own experience, it's one of the most effective ways to learn how to change the bad habits, face irrational fears, learn methods for handling arguments, and learn techniques to help you stay composed—even when you feel angry and reactive.

Now: back to M/s. If Master says something upsetting to slave, there is a risk the slave will shift their "internal dialog" (the chatter in their head) and begin to wonder about Master's intent. That's not a path Master will want to encourage, for if the slave senses Master's intent is not to serve the relationship, then slave may view this emotional upset as relationship-threatening. In the extreme, slave may perceive it as a breach of Master's contract to protect slave's emotional self.

Among the useful information available concerning emotions and emotional triggers I'd urge you to look up Katie Byron and *The Work*. I recommend her approach because it's based on learning to understand the "story" you tell yourself about who you are, who your partner is, and what the world is like around you. It's easier to control your reactions to events if you understand how you're perceiving those events in the context of the story that you tell yourself is true about your universe that others may see quite differently.

Maintaining connection

As I mentioned a few pages back, Mastery doesn't come gift-wrapped. You don't go to sleep one night and wake up a Master (unless you're doing this on the Internet, which—magically—*does* seem to produce quite a number of spontaneous "Masters." But I digress…). Actually, Aristotle pointed out, "Excellence is an art won by training and habituation. We do not act rightly because we have virtue or excellence, but we rather have those because we have acted rightly. We are what we repeatedly do. Excellence, then, is not an act but a habit." This applies equally to relationships.

In the long run, relationships (whether M/s or in other aspects of your life) live or die as a function of the *connection* that maintains rapport.

Relationships have their ebbs and flows, but unaddressed ebbs are risky: they indicate the existence of topics so relationship threatening you can't discuss them. These are the "elephant-in-the-room" issues that trigger one or the other of you. You've learned to live with each other without emotionally "flattening" them. One or the other of you has decided the emotional cost of trying to address the "real problem" is not worth the risk, so you've resorted to living together within the structure of your daily routines. A "chose your battles" mentality.

When close connection is replaced by routine and mundane interactions, the relationship risks transforming into something more closely resembling "business owner and employee." The businessperson retains the employee so long as the employee does their job adequately and does not cross any of the owner's boundaries; the employee remains with the owner because they're receiving what they judge to be fair compensation (and it's less work to stay than to go). The relationship is insipid, but tolerable. Translating this back into M/s, Master permits the slave to stay because of the practicality of the slave's service. The slave may stay out of financial necessity: I know of a number of cases where the Master required such life/work changes from the slave, they were essentially unemployable by the time the relationship foundered. In another situation, Master converted the slave into a *major domo,* with overall Household responsibilities. Master took beta slaves to replace lost intimacy with the established slave. Sometimes this works; other times it doesn't. As usual, it depends on the people.

But again, I've wandered off topic. We were discussing *connection.*

So, then, "How do you maintain connection?" you ask. "By living in congruence with your *intentions,*" I reply. In the Leather world, it's called *living authentically.* "That shouldn't be too hard," you say. "Not so fast," I reply: "It depends upon whether Master or slave really want to live with what the other person has authentically turned into over time." People change over the years, and what was "authentic" 5-10-15 years ago is unlikely to be quite the same "authentic" of today.

Now, at the risk of harping on this overmuch, I'll repeat: Master maintains the relationship connection by honoring their responsibility to act for the relationship's well being. When Master acts for the relationship's well being, they're ensuring their slave's needs are met. When slave's needs are being met, it opens the pathway for slave to honor Master's wants: they are giving a gift. Translation: Masters serve their slave as much as their slave serves them, but Master does so by ensuring the overall stability of the relationship.

Oh, you might note: when slave's offerings become *sacrifices* rather than *gifts*, you've got a problem, Houston. You're in a downward spiral.

Power as a concept

As mastery in the M/s sense is about power, I thought it would be useful to spend just a little time discussing different kinds of power. Just to keep this section from becoming a book in its own right, I've provided summary paragraphs in two areas: some of the more general bases of power, and some thoughts about the principles of power in relationships.

Basis of power

Social psychologists have developed ways to describe sources of power in order to assess how *power* works (or fails to work) in specific settings. In relation to the M/s dynamic, it's useful to know that one can lose power if they behave differently than someone in their position is expected to behave. If either Master or slave (each of whom has their own kind of power) radically violates the other person's expectations of behavior, the relationship can end on the spot. In one case, the slave of 14 years was given 24 hours to remove its belongings.

So, with that in mind, here are (very brief) descriptions of the more common types of power. I want to run through these before I focus on power issues within a relationship.

Positional power is given to a person by virtue of the office they hold or because of the relative position they have in a relationship.

Referent (or personal) power is based on charisma and interpersonal skills. People follow such a person because they admire their personal qualities; they gain satisfaction and prestige from association with someone who exudes power. This is the most common form of power in an M/s structure.

Expert power (obviously) stems from one's skill or expertise in some area. An expert may draw a following because they are so well known; some relationships develop this way. Bear in mind: when you put someone with expert power in a situation where they are not proficient, they no longer have power. Thus, the fact an expert has a fan base from which a partner has emerged gives no assurance that this expert will be any good at relationship management. Different expertise. Expert knowledge is not a transferable skill.

Reward power depends on the ability of the power-wielder to confer valued material rewards. As every parent knows, reward-based management systems fail because you run out of plausible rewards.

Coercive power is attained by using negative actions or words to force someone to do something they wouldn't normally want to do. It includes the ability to demote or to withhold other rewards. Coercive power tends to be the most obvious but least effective form of power as it builds resentment and resistance from the people who experience it. This, by the way, is why "punishment systems" are so counter-productive in M/s structures that rely on the slave's *willingness* to serve.

Principles of power in interpersonal relationships
I thought this was an interesting list because these topics tend to come into play when the relationship gets stressed.

Power as a perception: In the same way one's reality is based on one's perception, Master maintains power to the extent the slave perceives Master as powerful. Whether or not Master feels powerful, and whether or not others around the Master feel the Master is powerful is of no consequence once the slave determines (for whatever reason) the Master is, in fact, *not* powerful.

Chapter 2: Mastery

You can see ample examples of powerful people losing their power instantly through changed public perception. Just consider the loss of influence of any of the big names in the news once they are exposed for one scandal or another. Whether it's a pro-athlete, a high government official, or even a member of the European Royalty, their power evaporates in the instant they are perceived as unworthy of the power previously given to them. Conversely, some people become influential/powerful without intending to do so. What they do—usually selflessly for others—is such overwhelming evidence of their worthiness they are bestowed with power and influence.

Power as a relational concept: Power exists in every facet of relationships, of course. The issue, here, is often how much relative power Master or slave has relative to any given topic. If one equates *power* with the ability to influence another to do something they normally would not want to do, one can imagine any number of situations in which a slave with specialized knowledge or skills will lead the relationship, as needed.

In my own relationship, I have specific authority to instruct my Owner to seek medical care if I believe her decision *not* to seek medical care is incongruous with her own best interests or the best interests of our relationship. In such a case, I would be acting for the greater good of the relationship in my role as my Owner's protector.

Power as resource-based: Power struggles over resources can have a strong impact on an M/s (or any kind of) relationship. Resource struggles can concern whatever the couple feels they need to remain a successful and motivated couple. Commonly, these include such resources as money, time, or love/affection. While power struggles obviously intensify as resources become scarce, not all couples see the same resources as battle-worthy. For example, a polyamorous couple will likely have a different approach to "loss of time together" than will a non-poly couple. The poly couple incorporates "sharing my partner's time" into their primary relationship.

The principle of *least interest* and "dependence power:" The person with less to lose by leaving the relationship has the greater power within the relationship. This is especially true if they know their partner is highly marketable, views terms such as *love* and *commitment* differently from one another, or have an unnerving history of relatively short relationships.

Power can be enabling or disabling: People who combine clear and confident communication with practical leadership can generally achieve stable and nurturing relationships—whether M/s or other. That's hardly a surprise. Except... I've seen clear and confident communicators be surprisingly ineffective when working with their biological family and/ or with their own partner(s). Power used to enable relationships creates a vibrant dynamic; however, the opposite is also true. Dysfunctional or disabling communication styles can doom a relationship. Either a misapplication of power or poor communication wisdom can create a demand/withdrawal behavior pattern. In this pattern, one person makes a demand and the other becomes defensive and withdraws. It is not necessarily the Master who triggers this protective/withdrawal behavior pattern: I've seen it work both ways. This level of communication failure generally signals a serious schism between partners.

Power as a prerogative: According to the "prerogative principle," the more powerful partner can make and break the rules. This is informally phrased as: "It's great to be king." The more powerful person has the prerogative to manage both verbal and nonverbal interactions. They can initiate conversations, change topics, interrupt others, initiate touch, and end discussions more easily than those who give them power. Those with less influence must rely more heavily on social norms and customs (protocols) to guide their casual conversations.

However, this list of traits is also gender-bound to some degree, so let's look at the other side of the gender equation.

Female versus male Masters

Women are generally brought up to be sociable; they're used to living in a world of complex female thinking. Women commonly go shopping together, go to the restroom together, and belong to women-only social groups. Men are brought up with *things* (or *objects*) more than

Chapter 2: Mastery

with other men. Historically, they are socialized as problem solvers and—in the case of men who play sports—as team players.

I'd like to step out on a limb, here, and make an assertion based on my limited discussions about leadership with heterosexual M/s couples (led either by men or women). As this is likely to be a controversial perspective, I'll warn you in advance: what follows is just my opinion based on my own observations. (My own Master doesn't agree with some of this.)

I suspect that the way women are socialized within Western culture impacts the ways that they operate as Masters. Heterosexual female Masters seem to be more concerned (than heterosexual male Masters) about directing male slaves in ways that nurture the slave and specifically benefit the M/s relationship. I also have the impression male Masters tend more often to look at their slaves as people who can help get things done—and the things the male Master wants done are self-serving.

When I expressed this idea to an established female Leather Master, she quipped that in her experience, some male Masters have trouble overcoming their "manliness." She likened male versus female Masters as: "Lumberjacks versus brain surgeons." While I don't think this is gender-linked, I do think some people behave more one way than the other. (The "lumberjacks versus brain surgeons" phrase rattled around in my head for a few years and I finally wrote it down in my conference notes. Unfortunately, I don't recall who said it. If you remember saying this to me, please contact me and I'll add the attribution to the next edition.)

I first learned about another difference between male and female communication styles from an article by David Cunningham titled: "Break-Up Busting 101: A Crash Course in Saving a Relationship FAST!" According to Cunningham, men tend to make statements while women tend to negotiate. When men speak, it's often to obtain or distribute information. It's factual and fairly brief; generally, there isn't a hidden agenda. Interesting, I thought.

Cunningham said more. When women speak, they seldom speak directly: questions are frequently statements and statements are frequently questions. What men often believe to be casual conversation is actually intended as a form of *negotiation*. He provides this example: a man and a woman driving somewhere and the woman asks, "Are you hungry?" If he isn't particularly hungry, the guy is likely simply to say "No" without any follow-up question. As any woman reading this knows, the woman is now pissed off. She may even generalize this as yet another example that her man "doesn't understand her" or "doesn't hear her" or "ignores her." However, as anyone knows who has ever read James Thurber's *Walter Mitty* stories, he's *really* ignoring her, he's piloting a paddle-wheeler down the Mississippi at the moment and no, he isn't hungry, thank you. (If you haven't read *The Secret Life of Walter Mitty*, I recommend it to you. Written in 1939, it makes outstanding bedtime reading.)

By the way, one of the challenges (at least for some heterosexual female Masters) is how to remain feminine and retain dominance over a man who is expected by society to be a dominant.

Master morality versus slave morality

I spent some time looking up "morality" when researching *core values* for this book. Rather by accident, I stumbled upon a line of thought I'd not heard before. I think it's worth relating, particularly following the discussion of differences between female and male Masters.

As it happens, the issue of Master/slave morality was a central theme of some of Friedrich Nietzsche's works, especially the first essay, "On the Genealogy of Morality." Nietzsche proposed two fundamental types of morality: "Master morality" and "slave morality." He observes that while Master morality weighs actions on a scale of good or bad *consequences,* slave morality weighs actions on a scale of good or evil *intentions.* In practical terms, this means that while a slave values things such as kindness, humility and sympathy, Master values such things as pride, strength, and nobility.

That's a rather remarkable insight on its own, but Nietzsche then says "morality" must be interpreted in the context of a particular culture. That is, language, codes of conduct, social practices (dare I say *protocols?*) are affected/influenced by a tug-of-war between these two types of "moral valuations."

These ideas may help Masters and slaves better understand their partner's frame-of-reference. Nietzsche is saying that at the level of core values, those who identify as Masters and slaves are speaking from somewhat different perspectives. To be forewarned is to be forearmed: both Master and slave can benefit from this realization.

The eleventh essential for Mastery

In mountaineering, there is a well-established list called: The "Ten Essentials." *The Mountaineers*, (a Seattle-based organization) assembled the original "Ten Essentials" list in the 1930s for climbers and outdoor adventurers. For the sake of making a point in a few more paragraphs, here is the list:

1. Map
2. Compass
3. Sunglasses and sunscreen
4. Extra clothing
5. Headlamp/flashlight
6. First-aid supplies
7. Fire starter
8. Matches
9. Knife
10. Extra food

However, anyone who has ever gone on a hike of any length knows something is missing from that list. There is an "eleventh essential."

Toilet paper.

As humans, we like to make lists of things. There are qualification lists for practically every job/profession known to man. Sometimes, really obvious items are left off the lists. For example, although any checklist for getting paid money in exchange for work has to include a line-item called, "show up," I've never seen it included.

Similarly, while the Internet is full of lists about how to be a Dom/me or Master, it took Master Skip Chasey to figure out the key item absent from those lists but critical to the success of M/s relationships. I've come to refer to as "*The Eleventh Essential for Mastery.*" The statement is: "*Master understands and embraces the many paradoxes of M/s.*" I first read this line in the handout from Master Skip Chasey's 2003 workshop titled: "Priest in Black Leather: Mastery as a Spiritual Calling." It didn't make much sense at the time, but I've never forgotten it.

M/s is serious stuff. It's the land of relationship geeks just as BDSM is the land of sex geeks. M/s relationships blow up or are sustained based on the couple's understanding of (and ability to adapt to) the many paradoxes of M/s. (Master Skip is one of my Heroes, but he knows that.)

Being grounded

Being grounded means different things to different people. Personally, being grounded means that I understand my motivations, know the kind of kink that sings to my heart, know my core beliefs about BDSM and M/s, and know how to live peacefully with my Owner within an M/s structure.

However, there are many other aspects to being grounded. Other aspects include being fully present: physically, emotionally, and energetically. It means your mind is not wandering or pulling your energy elsewhere. Your heart and soul are not searching somewhere in the past or looking into the future. To be present in the moment is as easy as breathing yet devilishly elusive. Countless thousands of people spend considerable time and effort trying to quiet their minds and come present in life.

Slow yourself down; little things matter. Every smile and every step is important. You are a complex thing comprised of all these little things. Your power—whether as Master or as slave—comes from your own projection of who you are as expressed through all your actions.

Unfortunately, most of us have been well taught since childhood to close ourselves off from many forms of emotional expression. As a result, it's now difficult for us to live in the moment, for our minds race with judgments and considerations about what we *should* be doing or how we *should* be feeling. When we are not grounded, our minds wander off and create chaos. We lose things, lock our keys in the car, and make mistakes at the bank. On some level, those around us pay for our emotional flailing.

For some people, being ungrounded and unorganized is a way of maintaining control: our lack of focus keeps people around us off balance. When Master is ungrounded, slave may become anxious about Master. Seeing their slave upset, Master now has the opportunity to move in and help them. It's an old control trick. When we are grounded and finally decide to be fully present, we open ourselves to options and opportunities normally too subtle or too masked for us to recognize through the haze of our scattered minds. Focus makes our presence powerful. Tension levels drop; peace and serenity enter. Healing takes place.

Translating all this into M/s-speak, I'm referring to having a realistic understanding of who you are and what you offer to those around you. Master Skip Chasey, has captured this concept eloquently: "Suit up, show up, meet whatever comes up." To which he then adds a quote from one of his own spiritual teachers, Eli Jaxon-Bear: "With a quiet mind, an open heart, no agenda and taking nothing personally."

It's not about you, actually, but it takes a lot of maturity to absorb this. This takes focus and work. It takes sagacity.

Managing stress

One day when cruising around the Internet, I found this story. Actually, there are a number of versions, so I'm including here the version I liked best.

A psychologist walked around the room while teaching stress management to an audience. As she raised a glass of water, everyone expected they'd be asked the "half empty or half full" question. Instead, she inquired: "How heavy is this glass of water?" Answers called out ranged from 8 oz. to 20 oz. She replied, "The absolute weight doesn't matter. It depends on how long I hold it. If I hold it for a minute, it's not a problem. If I hold it for an hour, I'll have an ache in my arm. If I hold it for a day, my arm will feel numb and paralyzed. In each case, the weight of the glass doesn't change, but the longer I hold it, the heavier it feels." She continued, "The stresses and worries in life are like that glass of water. Think about them for a while and nothing happens. Think about them a bit longer and they begin to hurt. And if you think about them all day long, you will feel paralyzed – incapable of doing anything."

Message: It's important to remember to let go of your stresses. Master will want to train your slave not only to recognize when you're stressed, but have plans/procedures for de-stressing you. You can't lead responsibly when you're stressed.

"Why mention "stress" in a book on M/s?" you may ask. "*Anxiety* is the fuel of control." I answer.

Anxiety is one of the most common forms of psychological stress, and no one is immune from it. It ranges from mild to severe. Some need medication for it. Neither a stressed Master nor a stressed slave is fully in control of themselves.

A couple of ideas spring to mind: First, as my friend Brett (LTD on Fet) said one time, "As Master, you'll want to cultivate your slave's service aspects so they can take care of you. You'll want them to have certain skill, such as CPR certification, first aid certification, and so forth." By extension, you'll want your slave to be able to identify your stress level and develop stress-interventions to help you. Second, as Master, you are responsible for finding ways of reducing stress in your life. Stress reduction goes along with being present, mindful, and empathetic, some of the key concepts involved in advanced M/s structures.

Protocols and rituals

I realize many of you use protocols daily in your lives; I also realize many are strongly opposed to using protocols in any way whatsoever.

Chapter 2: Mastery

If you belong to the: "We don't use protocols" school of thought, please let me speak with you privately for a moment.

It's not that you don't *use* protocols; it's that you don't *name them* "protocols." You probably have ways you want your partner to cook certain foods, prepare your bed at night, or bring you coffee in the morning. These individual actions (protocols) combine to form the rituals of your life. These everyday actions help focus our attention and intent. Protocols can be your friend; I'm only suggesting you recognize them, label them, and use them to your advantage as bonding tools.

Protocols and rituals can help to make your world special. They can be used to elevate your daily activities from the mundane to something memorable. You can build protocols and rituals to celebrate anything in your life: waking up in the morning, being dressed and ready to go to work. Once at work, you can develop protocols to help you to mindfully begin your day while recognizing the very special M/s life you are privileged to live.

You can build actions of gratitude into your day; you can have protocols for recognizing fellow workers or panhandlers on the street. You're alive; you live in a free country; we're not at war; you have a home. Beyond that, you have a partner who is dedicated either to serve you or to protect and care for you.

What else do you want, exactly?

So, here is a mini-exercise: as Master or as slave, what actions would demonstrate your appreciation for their role in your life? Well… what do you value? Do you value a clean house? Do you value a clean car? Do you value a clean garage? Do you value orderly shelves and closets and bathroom cupboards?

Do you value the way your partner looks? If yes, then would you logically assume they value the way YOU look? If yes, then… how do you look? How's your hair? How're your clothes? How's your weight? When you come home from work, do you change your clothes as a tribute to the joy you hold for your partner?

Again, I warned you at the outset I'm radical in my approach to M/s. But remember this, as you drift off to sleep tonight: you only have so many days left alive. You have only so many days left to make memories.

But you know all this, yes? So: How's it going?

Okay. I'll step off my soapbox. I'll next discuss some theory about why one might really want to use protocols.

> Protocols are a daily affirmation of consent.

The ego is designed to fight change. Because "living in a structured relationship" is so unusual, you can design your own protocols to establish something to hold on to, to provide stability. You don't have to think about how or why you are going to do something in a certain way; you just focus on doing it. As Master Michael adds: "Protocols provide the safety and stability of a 'default set of actions and behaviors' BOTH for Master and slave, and this is invaluable in all aspects of M/s life."

Protocols help to reprogram your brain; they help you to create habits. Protocols don't merely define how you look on the outside, protocols help to shape how you think on the inside. Since protocols are the way Master wants this particular slave to do things, and since people are different from one another, protocols are person-specific. You might think of *using protocols in public* as a way of wearing your beliefs. This raises the question about building public protocols that don't freak out the vanillas yet provide the constant connection and bonding these kinds of relationships represent.

Protocols force you into the "act-as-if" structure. The structure of your relationship has everything to do with your mindset and the authority system you're using. For example, protocols will differ dramatically in the context of a Leader/follower team model, or in the context of a paramilitary/hierarchical model, or in the context of a Daddy/supportive model. The point is, you can build protocols into any authority-based relationship system and use them both to recognize the authority imbalance and to honor the relationship.

Partners in non-structured relationships (marriage or BF/GF) often strive for a power-equal relationship. In such environments, each partner has to put up with some of the petty idiosyncrasies of the other, as neither person has the authority to require the other to change their behavior: that's the deal. Although the way one person does something may annoy or bother the other partner, the rules of most authority-equal relationships require the annoyed partner to get used to the behavior they don't like.

> "This way of life is not for everyone. We are all trying to support you as you find out who you are for yourself. I didn't choose to be a slave, I uncovered that I was a slave. I'm just not interested in choosing to try to be anything else."
>
> —NurseV (slave to SenorJaime).

Unlike power-equal relationships, Master has undisputed authority over the s-type's behavior and actions. In that light, Master can build protocols and simply prohibit unwanted behavior and actions. At least theoretically, slave is motivated to limit its behavior and actions to those that please Master—and thus support the relationship. Although we're back to the "It's good to be king" model of M/s, we're also back to a couple living harmoniously.

The slave's focus on protocols tends to diminish as they become the person who behaves exactly as Master wishes. It's like having to study katas (practice forms) in martial arts. Wax on, wax off. You can't really fight effectively until the katas "go invisible" after hundreds or thousands of practice hours. It's the same with protocols. You first focus on creating the protocol *forms*, then you go through the stages of learning and adjusting them to fit who you are as a couple. Finally, they become part of who you are as a person. As Master Michael points out: "One will have come closer to Mastery when they are invisible."

Doing authority-based relationships well

To say something has been "done well" is subjective. To say that a Master is successful in their practice is also subjective. To me, a successful Master is one who, after many years of slave management, has learned to be a thoughtful, introspective, and visionary leader for that person. However, my view is based on my own archetype as "scholar" and is likely to be different from your view.

Not all people learn from their experiences. Some who have been in relationships for many years really haven't been learning much at all. While some people are able to build cumulative knowledge, others are stuck in a bit of a rut and tend to repeat actions and behaviors year after year. These people are undoubtedly well-meaning; it simply hasn't occurred to them to explore options and opportunities to change a relationship that is

"The SlaveMaster has no choice regarding what He must order a slave to do. Each choice must be in the best interest of the slave. It cannot reflect His own self-interest. A slave can only be BORN to One who has internally sworn to the universe that He will act ONLY in the best interest of the slave, forever, without question, and without compromise. That is an absolute necessity for a man to yield who he is to another, to be BORN. This is a real, and natural process. No person determines what works and what doesn't. It is in the nature of the creature being BORN. It is non negotiable, it is un-modifiable and immutable. There are no 'work arounds,' and no way to 'fool' any of the processes."

—SlaveMaster in his post on *BornSlaves*, July 26, 2014

okay as it is. And okay is okay; it's just not extraordinary. Extraordinary takes work.

So here's a question to chew on: "Can the person deny their own greed when it conflicts with their self-interest?"

This next section offers some topics for your consideration. They will only interest you to the extent you find them personally relevant.

Recognize of the kind of relationship you're in

Relationships are all different. No surprise there. However, because those of us practicing M/s are so wrapped up on discussing relationship theory and practice, we have opportunities not as available to people in unstructured relationships. As I've said before, people who enjoy authority-based relationships are really relationship geeks. We enjoy exploring ways we interact intimately with people. We build and modify our relationships based on conclusions drawn from long discussions about our respective wants, needs, hopes, and dreams. This happens naturally, as we're trying to figure out what in the world we're doing.

Understandably, husband/wife or BF/GF relationships are usually based on socially-directed *assumptions* about how couples should behave. The social direction comes from the ways couples are depicted in the public media. Let me use romance movies as an example. To draw an audience to see the movie, there has to be some "problem" needing resolution. That very structure sends a cultural message: relationships are fraught with problems. How do we know this? Well, nearly every movie we've ever seen shows us. Not only is there a "problem," the movie teaches us the key players think they are perfectly capable of solving the problem on their own. When is the last time you went to a movie and saw a couple having an argument where one person suddenly stops and says: "Okay. Let's stop. We're in a loop. We're telling each other the same thing over and over. We clearly have a communication problem. Let's just slow this down for a moment. Tomorrow I'll find three professional counselors we can evaluate to help us resolve this issue."

Of course you haven't. That's my point. In the movies, the emotionally hurting couples don't seek (or even consider) getting professional help.

Think of it! You have all these movies portraying supposedly wealthy and successful business people and rather than use readily-available helping resources as they would in their businesses, they just bull their way through. This, of course, leads to all kinds of outrageous farcical behavior intended to be suspenseful and amusing, if not funny.

However, all this "carrying on" is really sending a public message. The lesson is: *this is how relationship problems get solved. You have an emotional meltdown and become dysfunctional.* After all, what kind of movie would you have if they just called a "time out" and agreed to find a counselor?

As a result of such silliness, the general public thinks they know what they are doing inside their relationships because our culture provides subconscious models every day of our lives. Unfortunately, most couples are less likely to explore various ways their relationships could work *better* or *differently* because the concept of alternative relationship models doesn't occur to them. They're nuts, of course, but they think that we're nuts, so it's a draw.

So: here are some topics you might consider discussing with your opposite member...

Kind of structure: Have the two of you worked through the fundamentals of your relationship? How much nurturing is expected and offered? Do you agree about how you're using protocols to keep the unusual nature of your relationship always before you?

Intent and purpose: Why are you a couple; in what ways have each of you changed the path of the other person's life? What are you doing in this relationship with *this* person you couldn't do with *another* person? Do they know this? When you discuss this question, your partner may tell you they appreciate attributes you hadn't really considered. Knowing this may change your own actions and reactions in relationship-improving ways.

Delight in your partner's joy: Presumably, Master is taking care of slave's needs and slave is taking care of Master's wants. Presumably you both are living particularly joyful and complete lives. Is this true? If it is true, and you are joyful because your partner provides this joyful environment, what do you do for them? If you are *not* joyful, why are you doing this?

Gratitude: Gratitude is closely tied to the prior point, so the question is: How do you show gratitude to a partner who is the delight of your life? Does your partner share in your joy and express their gratitude to *you?*

Courage to do what's right and what is needed: An authority-based relationship gives Master the authority to *do the right thing* for him/herself and for the health and well-being of the relationship. Have the two (or more) of you discussed what each of you thinks *the right thing* is?

Opportunity to learn more about specific aspects of relationships: How are you as a coach? Ever read any books on coaching adults? What do you know about formal teaching and learning theory? Do you know how to be happy for no reason at all? Do you have mindfulness practices? There are wide-ranging opportunities for individual growth and development; M/s offers a fertile field to work on yourselves for the betterment of your union.

A Master/slave dynamic is a very, very rare beast. However, it's a beast that needs feeding. While relationships differ somewhat, you might consider feeding yours some *personal flexibility, ongoing learning*, and *experimentation*.

Watch for breadcrumbs

I collect breadcrumbs. I've been collecting them since I was a teenager. They all live in an ever-growing book titled: *If At First You Don't Succeed, Then Skydiving is Definitely Not for You: Aphorisms and Other Sayings Collected by Robert J. Rubel*. Currently, it's about 90 pages long with about 15 quotes per page: something over 1,000 entries. Because of this life-long hobby, I'm particularly attentive when I hear really profound ideas condensed into a few pithy words. Master Skip Chasey handily won the "succinct words" competition years ago. Here, printed with his permission, is a collection relating to *Mastery* in its various iterations. I've omitted quotation marks, but these are all his words.

Quotes from Master Skip Chasey.

You can hardly miss the references to Master Skip throughout my prior books. This book is no exception. Over my years of attending his classes, I have managed to record many pages of really pithy ideas and statements that, in turn, profoundly influenced my own M/s Path. I've decided to collect a number of them here rather than overload the body of the book by saying things such as: "As Master Skip puts it…"

I hope you enjoy his wisdom as much as I do and let some of these ideas roll around in your head for a few years, as I've done.

- Be willing to have your heart broken over and over again. Enter into every relationship: commit.
- "A slave is very often a dominant individual who chooses to be obedient." (An insight that Master Skip derived from a conversation with Master Steve Sampson.)
- Responsibility: the ability to respond.
  - Because slave complies with Master's orders, it is the slave who has most responsibility in the relationship. ("Do what I say" is subject to filters and distortions.)
  - Slave's commitment to obedience lessens personal responsibility because slave is responsible for obedience. However, Master is responsible for the results of the slave's obedience.
- Without truth, you can't have trust. Without trust, you can't have surrender. Without surrender you don't have a slave: what does that say about your Mastery?
- When you are present and mindful, you have a natural response ability: a natural responsibility.
  - Under the rules of D/s, Master can do whatever he wishes to satisfy his needs/desires.
  - Under the rules of M/s, Master can only act for the slave's highest good, so some of Master's needs and desires will be sacrificed to the relationship
- Consider wisely: What do you truly need? True needs are only food/water, clothing/shelter, and air; everything else is egoic

desire. So: what do you want and what are you willing to pay for it? Consider wisely: It will cost you everything.
- Freedom: A Master fully understands and embraces the paradox of M/s
  - In an M/s relationship, a slave gives up their freedom. By fully embracing their slavery, a slave feels freer than ever.
  - In accepting authority over a slave, the Master takes away the slave's freedom. In developing the slave, the Master helps slave to break away from misidentification facilitating self-realization and, ultimately, freedom.
- "Who slave really is" is not merely slave to X, but slave expresses aspects of itself through service to Master as a slave.
- Paradoxes thrive in M/s relationships: what you see isn't what's really going on.
- The past is regret; the future is fear. Living in the moment means you have to face what's going on in your world.
- If you can't find a day when you've spent the entire time happy, chances are that you've been stuffing your emotions.

This next group of bullets represents comments picked up at conferences either from classes or from discussions. Because I didn't know I'd ever want to reuse the phrase, I didn't record the speaker's name. If you recognize one that you believe you originated, write to me and I'll attribute it to you. I've attributed those that I could.
- "People who are into the 'what' seldom get to the 'why.'" Alternate phrasing: "Those who are 'living in technique' or 'living in the form, ritual, or protocol' of what they are doing may miss the why." M/s is based on living in the why.
- slaves have a passion to serve their particular Master. For most slaves, the satisfying part of the job is doing the challenging work: it's the hard work that makes it good.
- Most people rush into a relationship based on "I want/I need" as opposed to "I have this to give." This ties in to "inward" and "outward" directed people; it ties to "towards" and "away-from" personalities. The overall direction of an M/s relationship depends upon whether the couple are inward or outward looking. One isn't more right than the other, but until

the couple understands how their own motivations work, they'll have trouble defining their purpose.

- Masters tend to be rational; slaves tend to be emotional. This is not so much gender linked as tied to their respective roles. As Master is working at guiding the ship, Master tends to stay rational. As slave is feeding its passion, the slave tends to be emotional.
- "M/s creates the opportunity for the Family to work together under strong leadership towards a common goal."
- "Trust is an act of faith, and the defining characteristic of faith is certainty in the absence of evidence. In other words, trust is given before a dominant has proven himself, before the provision of any other evidence than the submissive's gut feeling. Once he has, and there is more tangible evidence to go by, it is no longer a matter of trust, but one of certain knowledge." *Absolute Lifestyle D/s* by J. Mikael Togneri
- M/s is based on living in the why: service to Master is the passion.
- "Within a successful relationship, sharing enables issues to be brought out the open, discussed, and understood so they can be faced together. That leads to the requirement that there be an agreement to solve problems rather than escape them." Jack Rinella, *Ties that Bind.*

Your public persona

Most of the challenge focuses on getting your relationship right. However, another portion (probably the more fun part) concerns your public selves. How powerful are you as a couple? Are you a Power Couple or are you invisible? Do you care? If you care, you might consider investing some time and effort into your public persona. (You might think of this project as *adding a kink skill.)*

We've all had the experience of being out somewhere and seeing a couple that clearly stands out. It may not have been immediately clear what caught your eye, but they seemed to be *connected* and *present* differently than couples around them. The couple created an unusual impact; they appeared somehow different from most couples you're used to seeing. You may have felt drawn to speak with them. You felt their magnetism.

Chapter 2: Mastery

How you speak, dress, and spend your time all interacts to create the image of who you are as a couple. *Who you are as a couple* is a conscious decision. It's Master's decision. Resources are plentiful.

I can't recommend one change over another, but these books have helped me:

- *How to Make People Like You in 90 Seconds or Less* by Nicholas Boothman (Using neuro-linguistic programming and a study of interpersonal communication from UCLA, Boothman explains how to quickly establish rapport to mold the initial 30 seconds of contact to your greatest advantage. This applies to business and social settings and is an advanced book about social skills.)
- *How to Work a Room* by Susan RoeAne (This book lays down the fundamentals for savvy socializing, whether at a party, a conference, or even communicating online. RoAne shows how to overcome the five roadblocks that keep most people from making new contacts: it hones your social skills for situations when your *impact* matters.)
- *What Every Body is Saying* by Joe Navarro (This book explain how to "speed-read" people: decode sentiments and behaviors, avoid hidden pitfalls, and look for deceptive behaviors. You will also be able to work out what YOU are projecting to your partner and all those with whom you come into contact.)
- *Leading With Questions* by Michael Marquardt (Marquardt points out that while our conversations may be full of requests and demands, all too often we are not asking for honest and informative answers. More than that, we don't know how to listen effectively to responses. In my own opinion, this book is the definitive guide for becoming a stronger leader by identifying—and asking—the right questions.)
- *Supercoach* by Michael Neill (Whether you want to powerfully impact the lives of the people around you or simply wish to create a deeper, more meaningful experience of being alive, this book contains techniques for changing your life and for assisting others.)
- The various books by John Bridges for gentlemen and for ladies about how to dress, behave, and react in public.

(These are timeless books about old-fashioned etiquette adapted to our modern times. I've used them when building personal protocols.)

You'll come up with many other resources as you explore these options. Actually, finding resources is much of the fun!

Subtleties of Mastery

Few of us are born leaders. Those of us born without this gift have had to learn it. Some of us do it better than others. This section offers some ideas to consider the authority dynamic upon which your relationship is built.

Establish a positive environment

An anxious slave is an upset slave. An upset slave will have trouble focusing on its service. When the slave has trouble focusing on its service, it's likely to act tentatively around you. There are some basic techniques Master can use to help slave remain grounded and to create a positive and supportive environment honoring the power-imbalance of your relationship.

For a paragraph or two, I'd like to explore "anxious slave" from an unusual perspective. Here's the setting: for this exercise, Master is a man and the slave is a woman. Master has an established home or apartment. Master and slave are in lust; they're having great sex and they love every moment they are together. Master decides to have the slave move in with him. Of course, his "stuff" takes up most of the house/apartment, so her stuff largely gets sold off, given away, or stored somewhere. Master, dominant that he is, has a certain way he likes his surroundings decorated and is very happy with the results he has already achieved. In the beginning, as the slave is focused on "learning Master" and Master's protocols, she is distracted from thinking about such things as artwork, furniture style, and neatness. However, the new relationship energy is fading, and she's starting to look around.

Chapter 2: Mastery

"Where am I?" she asks. "Where are *my* things?"

Men may not think very much about the physical context into which they've brought a slave. Masters, especially older Masters who have particular ideas about how their home should look, may not be very interested in sharing wall or floor space with their slave's possessions. Even after many years together, the house may exude Master's aesthetic tastes. Not much on display represents the slave's past. No, I'm not saying this is a good or bad thing. I'm pointing it out because the topic of this section concerns the slave's comfort level. Actually, the message is: people feel off-balance after a change of any kind. Depending on the nature of the change, their uneasy feeling can last a long time. In the case of traumatic violence, the person is usually changed forever.

As Master's will governs the M/s relationship, the slave may have to readjust to *change* more often than in a power-equal structure. On the topic of readjusting expectations, I have a book to recommend. Who Moved my Cheese (by Spencer Johnson, MD) is a book intended for those who may fear or resist change. It encourages people to see change as a blessing. It helps to show you the nature of "cheese" and the role it plays in your life.

The book is a parable. It's written about four mice (two couples) who live in a maze. They have very different problem-solving and interpersonal skills. Their lives and belief systems are built around the world in which they've found themselves. Although the cheese can stand for anything from health to relationships, most of us reading the story will see the cheese as something related to our livelihoods: our jobs, our career paths, or the industries we work in. The story's point is that we have to be alert to changes in the cheese and be prepared to search for new cheese sources when the cheese we have runs out.

If you take "cheese" as the initial bonding force in your relationship, then the message is: it's Master's responsibility to find new bonding forces to sustain the relationship over time. Dr. Johnson says that while there's no single way to deal with change, the consequence of pretending change won't happen is always the same: The cheese runs out.

Here are a few general tips for getting ahead of a change-induced crisis.

First, be sure your current environment is stable. What is the quality of communication within your Family? Does each of you truly listen to the other and understand their needs? Has Master clearly defied slave's roles and responsibilities in the relationship? Does the slave appreciate the role it is playing in Master's life?

Second, analyze the change. If there is to be a change, in what ways might this change alter Master or slave's future roles? In what ways might this change represent a change in the way Master and slave relate to one another: will this increase or decrease your time together? Will this change introduce someone into your dynamic who is likely to bring greater cooperation or introduce discordant competition?

> "Never waste a good crisis."
>
> —Secretary of State
> Hillary Clinton, 2009 quoted
> in *Time* magazine
>
> *******
>
> "Sometimes a crisis is an opportunity,
> sometimes it's just a crisis;
> some issues simply cannot be
> resolved."
>
> —Unattributable, but
> popularly quoted in relation
> to Mrs. Clinton's statement, above

Third, make contingency plans. As soon as you suspect *change* is about to pay you a visit, come together and plan. You'll not want to be planless when you bump up against a scary place, for once a crisis is upon you, your ability to plan is severely limited.

In essence, a stable environment is built around certain realities:
- You can't really control others (and what others will do with

anything you say to them); you can only control yourself and your reaction to events around you. (This is the difference between you happening to life or life happening to you.)

- Communication is the foundation of any relationship, and clear, consistent speech is the foundation of communication. (Communication clarity improves once you both know how you and your partner take in information: for example, do you need to get the feel for something, see how it works, or hear certain phrasing?)
- *Connection* is expressed through protocols and rituals; it's important to create opportunities for Master to express their authority and for slave to demonstrate their obedience.
- Since *what gets written down gets done,* Master is responsible for making time to have structured planning-and-review times with slave. (Master, as the Company's CEO, might think of these as *planning, evaluation,* and *review* opportunities.)
- Relationships thrive on happiness: Masters can create happiness in many ways, but one method I particularly recommend is to catch the slave doing things right and by expressing gratitude for what each of you brings the other.

Contentment is a close friend of happiness and contributes substantially to maintaining a harmonious relationship. Here is a brief list of attitudes I feel help me in this area; you'll have to create your own list.

- **Love what you do.** This seems obvious, but people frequently do things they're not very excited about. Find things you love doing and do them. If you have mundane tasks in your life, build protocols to turn those mundane tasks into lessons in mindfulness.
- **Help others.** There is always someone out there who is worse off than you are. Offer to help them; whenever possible, help people anonymously: think of it as building Karma. Helping others keeps you grounded; it helps to maintain your sense of proportion and balance.
- **Build relationships and trust.** Focus on building relationships both personally and in your work life. Since demonstrable trustworthiness also builds relationships, these two go hand-in-hand.

- **Be curious, be more interested than interesting.** When you're curious about other people, and about life in general, you tend to be a better listener, a better friend, and more generally informed about life around you. All this is good for your self-image. All this builds towards contentment.

On thanking your slave

In October 2013, my partner, Jen, and I spent the weekend in Phoenix, Arizona, participating in the marvelous "Butchmann's Experience." There, I heard something with far-reaching implications for any relationship; it certainly has had a profound impact on my own.

It concerns Master thanking his or her slave.

I realize some Masters consider their slave to be something like chattel, and one doesn't thank chattel for doing as they're told. I also realize other Masters believe "doing the job perfectly" is the standard, and you only thank someone for exceeding the standard. Setting those viewpoints aside for a moment, I'd like to address the actual words Master would use when deciding—for whatever reason—to thank their slave.

In English, a number of words and phrases have become social tropes: words that are used to fulfill a perceived public obligation but are really devoid of meaning. Examples include: "please" and "thank you" and "Hi, how are you doing today? Oh, great, glad to hear it." M/s couples have an interesting opportunity, here.

When you ask for something, you have been taught to say, "please." Of course, the full phrase is, "If it pleases you," however, you'd be shocked and offended if the person hearing your "please" suddenly paused to consider whether or not it would please them to pass you the salt. Similarly, lightly saying, "I love you" at the end of a phone call to your vanilla partner, sibling, or parent is often a phrase devoid of emotional commitment and meaning. It's *just the thing to say.*

For a moment, let's consider the ways Master might say, "thank you" to their slave. In a general sense, slave's purpose is to serve. It's their job. Do you, as Master, mean to be **asking** them to do something for you, or do you mean to *tell them* to do something for you? Personally, I believe that asking either weakens Master's authority or dilutes the intent of the relationship. Now, if Master is only *training* the slave for everyday service, it makes sense to let them know they have perfectly completed an order. In such a setting, the positive affirmation by Master helps to build their self-confidence and anchor their action as a *defined, repeatable process.*

However, if Master wishes to close off each order with a phrase communicating their mindful presence, I believe overused phrases such as "thank you" are your enemy. Such phrases fail to signal your mindful appreciation for the outstanding job completed by your special slave. You might consider substituting, "good job, slave" or "good slave" or "good boy/girl." These will be more meaningful (special; significant) to the slave than "thanks" or "thank you."

Before leaving this topic of English syntax, here's a tip for the slave: From Master's point of view, the phrasing: "Do you wish this slave to…" will be better received than, "May this slave…" In the first instance, Master retains control of the question; in the second case, the slave is expressing their will.

Men, women, and Mars

Master has all the power.

Of course: why else would Master be Master?

However, there is good use of power and there is misuse of power.

Slightly tongue-in-cheek, here are some descriptions of mostly-male afflictions. If they resonate with you, you probably have some personal work to do. I'm blunt. I'm 70.

Male Answer Syndrome: Men (far more than women) are socialized to solve problems and to fix things—preferably on their own. Men are expected to have an answer for almost everything. This is where MAS (Male Answer Syndrome) comes into play. Ask a man a question and you'll get some kind of answer. Obviously, whether the answer bears any relationship to being the *correct answer* depends on the question and the man.

MAS also crashes into conversations with their female partners when the woman is "venting" about something and makes the (dreadful) mistake of asking a rhetorical question. The Man, thinking He is being Asked for an Opinion (the farthest thing from the woman's mind at the moment) provides a Helpful Answer. This interjection triggers either dead silence masking anger, or an explosion somehow centering around the concept that You (the Man) are Clearly Clueless and don't ever *Listen* to Her. (Apologies for my *Winnie the Pooh*-like capitalization; I couldn't help it.)

GABH: Get A Bigger Hammer: Some men use the GABH approach to solve life's problems. When faced with a physical challenge, men tend to want to **G**et **A** **B**igger **H**ammer because *the problem* (whatever it may be) must (so they've been taught) yield to superior force. (This is conceptually related to the idea that working *harder* is working *smarter*.) *Raising one's voice* is the emotional version of the GABH approach to problem-solving. Some men feel they project more Authority and Control when they raise their voice. True for bullies; untrue for adults. A Master out of control is out of Mastery.

Problems arise when using the GABH approach with interpersonal issues. First, it gives rise to the idea that might makes right and that problems are nails requiring hammering. That cycle can lead to verbal abuse. Second, when you reach for a bigger hammer, you're less likely to catch *subtlety*. It's always a good idea to keep your ears open for *subtlety*. Remember: Master only knows what Master knows, but slave knows not only what slave knows but also quite a bit of what Master knows. Wisdom lies in heeding your slave's suggestions. To the extent that Master empowers their slave's "voice," the reaffirmed slave will feel they are contributing to the relationship.

If Master is afflicted with MAS or GABH behaviors, slave may conclude they need to find a more socially mature Master.

By the way, I suspect President Dwight Eisenhower was referring to a subordinate using the GABH leadership method when he was quoted saying: "You do not lead by hitting people over the head. That's assault, not leadership."

The Rescuer: This fellow is a cousin to The Fixer. Some people are called by their "rescuer" archetype; they are drawn to people they see as needing help. When someone with a rescuer archetype pairs up with someone with a victim archetype, the result is called co-dependence. Co-dependence is complex; it's largely subjective and can be hard to identify. Many books are written about it. Those with co-dependence issues probably need outside professional help.

Setting actual co-dependence aside, let's consider the situation in which one person helps another to solve a challenge.

Helpfulness is a positive trait that can turn negative based on the intent of the person offering to help. Rescuers differ from helpers: they don't ask permission to help, they simply thrust themselves into the situation and take over. The rescuer's ego demands feeding and "being helpful" provides good fuel. However, uninvited help has consequences. If you keep intervening and "helping" someone, how are they to learn another way? Your well-intended actions support poor problem-solving skills and (related) poor self-image. Test: have you been surprised when someone you "helped" resented your efforts?

To stay on the "helpful" rather than "rescuer" side of the table, there are a few questions to be answered before acting. First, is the person capable of solving the challenge? Not everyone is and your help may be welcomed. Second, did they ask for help, or are you stepping in without consent? Third, what makes you think you can solve the challenge any better than they can? Problem solving is another of those tricky areas: as people *think* differently, they also *problem-solve* differently. The results may be different than what you would achieve, but "different" does not make them wrong.

Managing your reputation

Your reputation can get tarnished by mistake. This started to happen to Jen and me. Within a few days of returning from an East Coast conference, I started seeing references about Bob and Jen on our local clubs eGroups. At first, it was hard to figure out who was upset about what. As the story quickly unfolded, Bob and Jen had been at a conference, and Bob was being admonished for not interrupting a scene in which the Top allegedly played through a "red." The rumor seemed to be taking off like a rocket. I called the president of one of the local clubs: they said yes, they had heard the story and were surprised I'd not interrupted the scene.

Well, I was nonplussed: we hadn't attended the conference play party the prior weekend. We had not played at all; we hadn't watched anyone playing.

She promised to look into it. About three hours later, she called me to say, "It's a small, small world" and went on to explain. There is another "Bob and Jen" couple in Austin, and THEY had been to a *different* conference and had *attended* a play party during which someone allegedly played through "red." The entire mess was a nothing, and it never happened and yes,

> To perform a reality check on your Mastery, leadership skills, and reputation, imagine you have a terminal illness; you have only two months to live. Now, ask yourself this: "Are you the kind of Master you'd recommend to your own slave?"

she'd contact the other club presidents and explain. Thank you, Rose. (I know and like the other "Bob and Jenn" couple. Known Bob for years. And, while they were in the room where this took place, they were not watching it. Rumors.)

Chapter 2: Mastery

So: what am I getting at? This: *Reputations are history in rumor form.*

Little missteps get repeated and attach themselves to other reports of missteps. Over time, a person gets tagged as a "this" or a "that." And, it can be *very hard* to correct your community's impression of you. You may try to explain things, ask for meetings with your community leaders, write rebuttals all over Fet, but your reputation remains in the gutter. This happens for a variety of reasons.

- What you're being accused of is "not good form" within our culture and being associated with the stink makes you an outcast.
- You're not being accused of anything specific, but the general impression people have of you is not positive. Here, the challenge is to find some way to alter your public's perception of you, for—as every advertising executive knows for absolute certainty—perception is reality. As Arthur Lenehan pointed out some years ago, "Reputation grows a like mushroom; character like an oak."
- Our brains want good stories and they put things together that have only faint relationships to reality.

For those of you who are interested in developing a method to iron-coat your reputations, I'd direct you to read (or reread) Stephen Covey's marvelous book: *7 Habits of Highly Effective People.* Within his book, I'd draw your attention to the distinction between "personality ethic" and "character ethic." As Covey points out, the culture of the US has shifted away from "character ethic" over the course of the last 75 years or so, much to our detriment. You might wish to consider where your own values stand in relation to those two very different approaches to "being" in the world.

Chapter 3: slavery

slaves have to grapple with certain *truths* or *realities* as we settle into this edgy and unorthodox position.

First, we understand that we have committed to absolute obedience. We have committed to following both to the letter and the spirit of any ethical order from Master. We realize that the quality of our slavehood (a cute word, yes?) relies on our own integrity to put our wants second to Master's wants. The quality of our slavehood depends on our ability to turn over to Master responsibility for meeting our needs, however Master interprets them.

Second, many M/s couples consider M/s relationships to be a *calling*. It's a calling because we just can't imagine living any other way even though we realize our lives are radically different from most

---

"There is no such thing as partial slavery. We live as we must live, in moral certainty (and without the possibility of moral failure), or our slavery isn't granted to us. Our slavery remains a moving target that we can't reach without unqualified surrender to obedience."

—SlaveMaster, as posted on Bornslaves.com Feb 13 2014

Chapter 3: slavery

husband/wife relationship models. We think vanilla relationships are probably okay for *them,* but that's because *they* just don't understand the depth of connection and communication we get from our structure. We feel they are missing the benefits gained from living in a focused, mindful relationship.

Third, it's hard to get objective help from outsiders. Since "slavery" is not socially accepted, licensed professionals will have to overcome their own culture and personal biases to speak with us. Furthermore, since they wouldn't understand *our* culture, how can we go to them in the first place? As a result, those from whom we are most likely to turn for help are, themselves, tainted. They are tainted, because they, too, live in the world of authority-imbalanced partnerships, so they must share our distorted sense of how relationships should run. (This is the logic underpinning the old Groucho Marx joke, "I wouldn't want to join any organization that would accept me as a member.")

Fourth, and more seriously, for the relationship to last, slave has to get as much fulfillment as Master. That requires both good leadership and good followership (look, another cute word).

There is a lot of material in this book speaking to the "leadership" side of the equation: this chapter is for those who are following.

Since I became part of what might be called the "national kink conference presenter circuit" and been able to attend dozens upon dozens of conference presentations by established Masters (and had interactions with hundreds of people attending my own presentations), my understanding about differences between D/s and M/s has grown deeper.

About two years ago I arrived at what I thought was probably the key distinguishing characteristics of M/s structures. Said in one sentence: *Ownership* distinguishes a "slave" from a "submissive."

If you've stayed with me to this point, then the next step won't be so hard: the thing about *property* is it's always ready to be used. Not sexually, (that, too) but in the sense it doesn't have to "check in" with someone else to be sure it's available. As with everything you own, your property (including your slave) agrees to do whatever you ask within the limits of its capabilities. This means the camera will agree to take photos, your filled scuba tanks will agree to give you oxygen, and your chair will agree you may sit on it. The common thread, here, is that everything you own (kept in working order) would (if it could speak) say "yes" to any request even before you asked it to do anything. So: as someone who wishes to acquire property to use in a certain way, it is your responsibility to obtain the correct piece of property. You can't expect a film camera to produce downloadable jpg files. If you want to make a silk purse out of a sow's ear, you have to start with a silk sow.

This idea of "pre-authorization" brings up the concept that the real flesh-and-blood person who signs up to be *property* has given their Master a *blank check* (as SlaveMaster phrases it). slave has given prior consent to perform any task asked of it for which it has the skill and training. Henceforth, I refer to this total "consensual pre-agreement state" using SlaveMaster's term: "blank check."

So much for the conceptual background; now, on to the body of the chapter.

How do you practice your slavery?

Slavery is about optimizing Master's world according to Master's preferences/priorities. Okay. We can agree on that: but how do you do it?

Miriam-Webster's Online Dictionary defines *ready* as: "properly prepared or finished and available for use; almost about *to do* something."

The same source defines *willing* as: "not refusing to do something; quick to act or respond; doing something or ready to do something without being persuaded."

As it happens, a recent string of posts on *BornSlaves.com* brought up the distinction between *being ready* and *being willing*. rocky67 posted a line that I thought hit to the heart of the matter. He said: "After reading the definitions of ready and willing, this slave thinks we must first become ready and then put it into action. It would like to learn more about how to convert its readiness to willingness."

Converting readiness to willingness.

What a thought. Thank you rocky67.

We're back to the blank check.

"The first rule of service is this: it's not service unless the master wants it.

This is the conflict between serving Master as Master wishes

Versus serving Master as you would like to be served if you were Master.

So long as Master wants it, all service should be seen as valuable."

—Raven Kaldera

Willingness is expressed by walking the walk; rolling with the punches. *Willingness* means transmuting your service into joy; under-promising and over-delivering. *Willingness* means serving with a good attitude, and that means serving without negative self-talk. Negative thoughts (almost by definition) directly defy the way your Master wishes you to think about yourself. So, stop it.

"Ah!" you say. "There's another of your quips so easily typed out at 8:27 on a Tuesday evening! How in the world do you stop thinking negative thoughts about yourself?"

So glad you asked. I have some suggestions. Perhaps the quickest way is to read a book titled: *What to say when you talk to yourself* by Shad Helmstetter. Frankly, *all* of his books are life-changers, and I recommend them without reservation. In addition to Shad's books, I also am very enthusiastic for the work of Gary van Warmerdam. Found on the Internet, his course is called: *Pathway to Happiness* (www. PathwayToHappiness.com). If you are seeking permanent personal change, take the course. Oh, you can't just listen to his course; you have to do some things. To change your self-talk, van Warmerdam offers this clever tip: Thoughtfully write a long, long, long, long, long list of attributes you or *your Master wished you exhibited.* Try to write down 100 or so desired attributes—you know, things like...

- "I unfailingly use 'active listening' when speaking with others" (*Active listening* means you speak back to the other person the essence of what they just said so they can agree you heard them correctly or restate more clearly what they intended to say.)
- "I smile all the time, for I know others will see my smile and think positive thoughts."
- "I am thoughtful about how I walk; I walk with correct posture and exude self-confidence."
- "I remember everything Master says to me and I act on those recollections."
- "I exercise *portion control* during every meal."
- And on, and on, and on.

Write out everything positive you think you aren't. The next process is to start feeding this material back into your brain. You do this by using any computer-based audio-recording program (such as Garage Band on the Mac) and a little plug-in microphone. Record your own voice saying all these positive, wonderful things to you about who you are. You can turn it into an audio file and transfer it to your smart phone. Now, play it to yourself as much as you possibly can (when driving, when exercising, when doing housework…).

Over time. Over time. Over time, it will change you. You'll be amazed.

Oh; it doesn't hurt to put positive affirmations all over the house, too. However, that's a discussion to have with your Master.

Why are you a slave?

Many of us have been surprised to awaken one day and find ourselves to be "slaves." While some of us sought this position, others felt we didn't have a lot to say about it. For those in this second group, some of us felt trapped; others felt as though we'd answered a *call* that, in itself, clarified a part of who we are.

From my own experience, the *call* behaved much as a light switch: I went from "off" to "on." Actually, it happened with an e-mail from my Leather brother, slave mikey. One minute I thought and behaved one way, the next minute I didn't. And my chattering mind went quiet; it's stayed quiet to this day. (This was *very* confusing to those who knew me during the transition. It was particularly confusing to Jen, who suddenly felt me push through the last wall of resistance and crash onto her lap. It took about another full year for her to believe I had, in fact, embraced my slaveheart. Unfortunately, some of the emotional damage inflicted before the transformation still lingers.)

Once one surrenders to *the call,* they often find themselves touched by a passion to find a worthy Master/Mistress—even as they recognize D-types are also *fallible people.* It can be a challenge to establish the level of trust required to enable slave to "release" to Master. Let me take a paragraph to explain how the "light switch" of release worked for me.

Having come to Jen from owning a slave for the prior eight years, I found it jarring even to consider surrendering control over my personal time and my ability to plan for my own future. Jen and I had many serious upsets over these topics, as well as issues about my natural dominance. We tried a number of structures before venturing into M/s, but M/s worked the best for us. After living together for over two years (and watching how she managed our upsets), I ultimately concluded that she could probably manage me better than I could. Also I realized how much my experiences with her had already improved my life. These realizations came as a flash of insight. I reacted by tearing a check out of my checkbook, filling it out, signing it and—quite literally—handing it to her. I thought the symbolism was important: this was my way to demonstrate willingness to answer "Yes" to anything she henceforth asked of me.

Now, if you also believe this way, then here's the rest of the story: the move from *submission* to *slavery* involves *closing the door after yourself, forever.* You are no longer in command of yourself. You have no free time, and all your efforts are at Master's direction. At least, some people look at it this way.

Bear in mind, declaring yourself to be a slave is something like graduating from college and starting a graduate program. You now have to master the many and complex aspects of a very unusual, complicated, and cerebral relationship structure.

- At some point, most relationships shift from hot sex and newness into *devotion;* few attain absolute commitment.
- Ultimately, there is only one decision: you will or will not put 100% of your trust in this person. If yes, then your sole obligation is to live in obedience.
- slave's mastery centers upon taking responsibility for obeying. Any violation represents a failure to live in authenticity in integrity.
- Submission without dominance occurs when you continue doing what you think your Master wants even though they insist they don't want it.
- Dominance without submission occurs when Master keeps telling you to do something and you keep telling Master, "No" or thinking to yourself: "This is BS, do it yourself." (Actually, what slave is likely to think is: "Of course I'll do it, but you're squandering my brilliance and initiative. You don't seem to know what you have in me.")
- Submission is about direction of behavior; surrender is about alignment of will. Surrender is routed in the spiritual realm.

"If my Master is lost, I'll find him. I'll lead him back to himself, because to serve doesn't always mean to follow."

—Joey W. Hill, *Hostile Takeover*

Obeying

Obedience means to conform to the explicit instructions or orders from an authority figure. Obedience is generally distinguished from *compliance* (going along with peer-supported rules/customs) and from *conformity* (behavior matching accepted social norms). Obedience can be seen as immoral, amoral, or moral depending upon the situation. For example, while "Person A" killing "Person B" in a non-wartime civilian situation is considered immoral. However, "Soldier Person A" killing "Enemy Person B" during wartime is considered moral. This can get tricky, of course, but that's what Grand Juries are for.

In the context of authority-imbalanced relationships, one *develops* obedience. It's a discipline. Obedience is grounded in a slaves' repeated experience of trust from their specific Master. There's another way of looking at *obedience*. You can look at it as an ongoing willingness to choose to remain in the relationship. After all, the slave is only responsible for its willingness to choose; Master is responsible for empowering the capacity for the slave to obey. In practical terms, this means (as I've previously mentioned) Master may give orders to test the slave's willingness, but Master should not give orders to test the slave's abilities. Master is responsible for ensuring the slave has all the abilities it needs to serve as Master wishes.

Now: There is a big difference between a slave obeying and a slave simply agreeing.

This difference between obeying and agreeing relates to a person's self-image as much as it relates to a person's self-control. Self-image is strongly influenced by whether they are internally or externally motivated as well as whether they are self-validated or externally validated. Master Michael adds that this issue about obeying and agreeing also concerns internal and external alignment. "Simply agreeing," he points out, "may really be a neutral position for the slave while they wrestle with the larger question about whether or not they will obey this Master."

Translation: as a human being, nature has bred us to take care of ourselves, to check in with ourselves about whether one or another action is in our own best interests. However, this trait of *checking everything against our own understanding of our own best interests* can block slave's submission. In psychology, it's called *sorting-by-self.* You interpret what is said to you and what others do in relation to how you feel about it. This can hurt you as a slave: analysis can obstruct obedience.

"Obedience is not what we do; it's an essence...a condition of being in a state of non-judgment, non-evaluation, and non-attachment" observes Raven Kaldera. He goes on to say: "Obedience is the linchpin of an M/s relationship; obedience is *absolute commitment to Master's authority.*" (I strongly urge you to read everything Raven Kaldera and Joshua Tenpenny have written about Master/slave relationships. Their books are listed in the Supplements. They are profound thinkers and outstanding writers and presenters.)

I've discussed *alignment* (or obedience) in some depth with my Leather brother, slave mikey (Fet=slave-mikey) and his profound comment on the topic is: "Struggle and suffering only happen in non-obedience." So: the challenge is to get to alignment—through obedience!

There was quite a bit of discussion about obedience during *The Butchmann's Experience* weekend Jen and I attended in 2013. SlaveMaster remarked, "Obedience is not agreement or compliance. You find obedience by recognizing what it's not." (I thought that was a pretty elegant observation, and it brought to mind a quote by the great sculptor Michelangelo Buonarroti (1475-1564): "Every block of stone has a statue inside it and it is the task of the sculptor to discover it.")

SlaveMaster went on to say, "*Developing obedience* is an experience. Master is responsible for empowering the slave's capacity to obey, but a slave is only responsible for the willingness to choose: Master's responsibility ends with the slave's lack of willingness. slave must be willing to say 'yes' before the question is asked: mentally, the slave must offer Master a blank, signed check." Reinforcing this point, SlaveMaster added: "The magic only comes when the 'yes' comes before the order."

For Masters who are reading this section of the book, I'll add another comment from SlaveMaster: "In building trust, you start with small orders. When we explain an order, it's because the relationship is new, because the significant orders in our life come from giving orders without the cerebral backup and have them followed. Establish trust through explanation, but once established, slave must trust all orders without asking for explanations."

A slave who gives itself permission to do wrong—to lie or to be deceitful—can't hear its authentic self.

Were you aware it was an order?

Familiarity can lead to casual communication, and casual communication can undermine your structure. It can lead you back to Vanillaville. "Please bring me a Coke" can lead to a reply such as: "Sure." This is a world away from an exchange starting out: "slave, please bring me a Coke" followed by "Yes, Master."

It's comfortable to speak in this relaxed way, but it risks slave missing the intent of the sentence. It also risks Master feeling ignored even as the slave carries on unaware Master had just given an order. Here's an example from my life: Master says, "I'm going to take my shower now and get into bed." I reply: "Yes, Master, I'm just finishing up in the kitchen; I'll be there as soon as I can."

I, an Aspie with a compulsive neatness streak, will **not** hear that statement as: "boy, stop cleaning up and join me in the shower, I wish to spend some quality time with you in bed." I had not heard Master's words as any kind instruction to stop cleaning the kitchen and living room. I only heard Master's words as a statement of her intended actions for the next 10 minutes or so. You can imagine my shock and sadness when, upon taking more than 10 minutes to finish cleaning the kitchen and showing up in bed after my shower, she commented about the loss of quality time together..

It can be hard to change from casual speech, because we spend our workdays speaking casually. We're used to it. However, I believe it works against your M/s dynamic. To avoid this situation, Master may wish to develop certain speech protocols. One such protocol is to require the slave always to use "active listening." Active listening involves the hearer repeating what the speaker said to confirm they heard the speaker's intentions as well as the words. Protocols such as these are tricky: this is an area where individual preferences determine the solution.

Submission versus service

NOTE: I'll begin this section with a warning of sorts: this section is written from my personal perspective and contains definitions and descriptions I have developed over the last few years to help me make sense of our M/s world. Some people go along with these distinctions; others don't. Ultimately, what I think doesn't matter and what you think does matter. I can only offer you my viewpoint: you have to adapt what works and leave the rest for another time.

There seems to be some confusion about being a slave versus being a submissive. I have the sense many people think of a slave as someone who is really a super-submissive. To this day, I hear people say, "I couldn't be a slave; I'm too dominant." This keeps many potentially good slaves away from considering such a role for themselves. I suspect this attitude is influenced by one's self-image. Some resist being a slave because they don't see themselves as submissive. Frankly, I think this confusion results from not having worked through D/s versus M/s roles.

As you've already realized, I consider the words "submissive" and "dominant" to be context-linked personality descriptors that vary depending upon specific situations. One may be submissive in one setting and dominant in another. Basically, a slave's role concerns *service and obedience.* "Service" is meant both in the general sense (*Chop Wood, Carry Water: A guide to finding spiritual fullfillment in everyday life* by Rick Fields and Peggy Taylor) and in the specific sense (*The Art of the Table: A complete guide to table setting, table manners, and table wear* by Suzanne vahn Drachenfels).

I'll go further: frustration over role expectations can end a relationship. I picked up this comment from one of my workshops: "When you first realize that the relationship isn't going to work out, you feel you've flunked the slave test."

If such thoughts have crossed your mind, then this section is for you.

I am sometimes asked whether I'm a submissive, as I am Master's slave. I reply that I am a dominant man in obedient service to Master and let them make of it what they will. If they push, I further explain that after two years of introspection and counseling, I concluded that Master could create a better future for me than I could create on my own. That tends to stop people. Am I submissive to her? Of course. Am I submissive to people in general? No.

As many of you have heard me say in lectures: serving in obedience does not alter your place on the "dominant-submissive personality scale." I think you'd have to look long and hard to find a priest who thinks of him or herself as submissive, yet they serve and obey others higher in authority within the church structure. In the military, you'll have quite a hunt to find a Lieutenant General who considers him/herself submissive to a Major General. These people have chosen to serve and obey someone (or some concept) in whom they have vested superior authority.

This line of reasoning brings us to ask: what does an M/s relationship structure, a religious hierarchy, and military rank have in common? To my mind, these are all situations in which people have committed themselves for some purpose and pledged to serve and to obey. In M/s, slave has pledged to Master and Master has pledged to the relationship. They are both in service.

How is this distinct from a D/s structure? For some, it isn't; for others, it is. Personally, I make most sense out of the "submissive/slave" argument when I introduce the word "ownership." Slaves are owned property, and submissives are something else. I don't care what that *something else is;* it's just that they don't generally think of themselves as property.

You are either owned or you are not. Where you fall on the Dominance-submissive personality scale is not relevant in my world.

Did you ever wonder whether your cell phone or car or bed are dominant or submissive? Laughable of course; they're property. And, they always do their best to serve you perfectly. What more can Master ask of a slave?

Withholding commitment

While some of us delight in the edginess of thinking of ourselves as an "owned slave," merely a piece of property, others aren't so quick to embrace the words, let alone this condition. Some seem to believe we're playing in a 21ˢᵗ Century land of make-believe and we're really free to reassert our autonomy if we conclude Master is taking advantage of us (regardless of any signed "contract").

All true, I suppose.

Really, though, most of us are simply trying to find someone who will love us and appreciate what we do for them; we are offering to dedicate ourselves within a committed relationship. I get it.

I also understand Masters have feet of clay and they sometimes annoy us so much we reach the point of actively resisting orders. Actually, this brings up a really important issue; the issue of withholding commitment to Master. From reading various posts on Fetlife's M/s groups, I realize that many slaves react to their Master's unwise decisions by limiting their own obedience. They only obey to the extent they trust their Master's intentions. This is *conditional* slavery, of course; slavery by slave's rules.

Being right versus being obedient

The need to be *right* in contrast to being *obedient* can put a slave at risk of offering only conditional service. This is Raven Kaldera's concept that has helped in my own M/s dynamic. I've learned to follow Raven's catechism when I feel reactive to some discussion involving Master. It starts from a question: "Why is being *right* in this situation so important to this slave?
- Was it the principle of the situation, or
- Fear of a bad outcome, or
- A struggle with priorities, or

- Past training, or
- Something else?"

Raven suggests other probing questions:
- *Who has the stronger emotional investment in the situation?* Do you really *care* about this topic or are you trying to make a larger point in your relationship? For example, have you been working very hard on the topic under discussion and know you're right and are upset at having to concede to Master's irrational insistence that you are *not* correct?
- *How do you each feel about how the situation worked out?* Were you able to work through the situation without an emotional meltdown? Have you established protocols to do this (talking sticks, for example)?
- *How would you feel if it had worked out differently?* I know, a loaded question. In my experience, when Master and I start to engage emotionally—particularly in some field where I believe I have a lot more experience—she withdraws emotionally and we try to end the evening as quickly as possible and get into bed. Nightly, we do word puzzles in bed and I read to her. By terminating the upset (even while we're upset) and going to bed where we have consistently positive experiences (protocol-based) enables us to defuse about any level of upset.
- *What's your reaction to finding out you (as slave) were wrong in the situation?* Are you relieved or annoyed?
- *What factors might pressure Master to give in, even if they don't want to?*
  - Clear evidence they are wrong?
  - The slave's distress?
  - Wanting to see the slave happy?
  - Something else?
- *Within your relationship, what are your priorities and goals in the situation?*
  - Obedience?
  - Reaffirming your dynamic?
  - Optimizing the outcome?

What tools can each of you use to achieve a positive outcome the next time you have a disagreement? Actually, how do you find out about relationship tools you might wish to add to your toolkit? If you want relationship tools, you have to hunt them down and master them to be sure they're accessible when you need them. Some tools are better in certain situations than others, and some tools can be outgrown. Actually, whether or not you use relationship tools at all depends on your personalities: Master may think they don't need "tools" to manage stress. They'd be wrong, of course, but that's beyond the scope of this book.

If you appreciate relationship tools, then here's one I think is spectacular and relevant just at this point in the book. In my opinion, it's well worth the money: *www.udemy.com/conscious-listening.*

Adapting

Issue: You've been in the relationship for some time. You've both changed in some ways. Master has become a little more tolerant here and a little less tolerant there. Change is afoot; change is always afoot. The question now becomes: "What knowledge, skill, or behavioral change is Master starting to look for, and do you have the capability and will to comply?" I've known of cases where the Master outgrew the slave, and I've known of cases where the slave outgrew the Master. This can be a challenging dynamic to keep stable over time.

When Jen and I began our relationship, we were extremely unstable. We are both strong dominants and we clashed over most things. It was difficult to find a structure that could stabilize us. We tried Mommy/boy, traditional Master/slave, no-structure, double-Dom/me, and something we called "Keeper/mess." They all failed.

Then, Raven Kaldera rescued us with his "Leader/manager" model. Now, Master says: "The goal is "X" and the success parameters are "Y" and "Z" and off I go. In business-speak (my own language) it's a "CEO/COO" structure. Master/CEO provides the direction and responsibility and then steps back. I am accountable for the success of the undertaking, whether it's dinner or a weekend trip.

Back to my lead question: "What kind of slave does Master want and is it consistent with what you can offer?"

Reacting to Master's authority

We all react. We react to the sun shining; we react to the sun *not* shining. We react to Master's smiles; we react to Master's frowns. Your ability to master your own reactions is referred to as "state management" by the NLP crowd (Neuro-Linguistic Programming). I go over a good deal of this in my earlier book, *Master/slave Relations: Communications 401—The Advanced Course.* There, I also discuss tricks to control your own reactions when you are "triggered." Here are two established techniques; this is not the place to go into more depth than this:

- Visualize the triggering incident: give it a color, shape, and texture. Hold it in your hand and shape it. Pet it. Now, in your other hand, envision your last orgasm. Feel it's warmth and excitement, remember how the room looked, how you felt. Now, take both your hands and clap them together. As you do this, say: "Swoosh" out loud or to yourself. That technique, alone, should make you feel better.
- Immediately upon being triggered, shift your mind to things for which you are grateful. You can start by being grateful you don't live in a war-torn country and work your way up to being grateful for having a home to live in, electricity, a phone, etc. There are great resource books and websites on gratitude; too many for me to select a single one. In a general sense, there are three guiding principles:
  - o Write down things for which you are grateful. Multiple studies have shown it to be more effective to write them out explicitly rather than only to think of them.
  - o Write with depth. Write at least five lines for each subject rather than one line about five topics. For example, if you're thanking Master for providing for you, go down the line and also thank Master for the food you cook, a means to cook the food, the appreciation he/she shows for your cooking, the cookware you're using, the place setting for dinner, etc. Think more deeply about how fortunate you are to have such a giving Master. Writing quality (how you express your gratitude) matters more than how much you write.

o It's important to focus mindfully on present and past events in which Master has made your life better for you. Your understanding of past and present events will help you shape similar future events.

Continuing with our question about how you react to your Master's authority, I'd ask: What approach do you adopt towards the person in authority? Do you *always* say, "Yes, Master" and serve as instructed? Do

> "When upset or angry, I get down on the floor and am upset at Master's boots."
>
> —Quote heard in one of my seminars

you take time to consider whether you've given Master all the information needed to make a particular decision? Before replying to Master, do you use "active listening" and summarize your understanding of what Master is saying?

Said slightly differently, do your responses to your Master nurture their authority? Can you actually list personal methods you have adopted to demonstrate obedience to Master's authority? Have you developed techniques to suppress possible reactions to Master's requests in order not to appear resistant?

Stuff to think about, anyway.

Managing emotional conversations

The popular phrase "emotional hijacking" describes the condition during which a person's emotions blind them to reason and logic. It is usually referred to in the context of aggression or fearfulness. Transactional Analysis recognizes this highly emotional state and refers to the speaker as using their "child voice," filled with emotional words.

Chapter 3: slavery

Actually, there are some really fascinating resources if you're interested in learning how to change your reaction to people around you.

- All three of Suzette Haden Elgin's books (in the *Gentle Art of Verbal Self-defense* series) are easy to read and filled with insights and techniques.
- Karla McLaren marvelous book: *The Art of Empathy: A Complete Guide to Life's Most Essential Skill,* (and her Internet-based audio learning program) presents in-depth information on empathy, emotions, and the empathic skills to help you develop and support healthy empathy in yourself and others (see: *http://karlamclaren.com*).
- In the shameless self-promotion department, you might consider my book: *Master/slave Relations: Communications 401—the advanced course* for the discussion about TA, Transactional Analysis. If you've become emotionally reactive and have dropped into *child voice,* Master's response in *parent voice*—the sound of *authority*—will likely make matters much worse. You (and your Master) need to know how to shift to *adult voice* to head off an emotional meltdown.

  Here is an example of an exchange where Master adroitly shifts into *adult voice* to head off an emotional exchange. This exchange works, because slave feels heard: slave will recognize that Master may choose not to agree with slave or do as slave wishes.
  "Master, you're not listening to me."
  "slave, it's not that I'm not listening to you, it's that I don't agree with you."

These (and other) resources can help you to develop skills to identify and neutralize emotion-laden topics and help you regain self-control.

Oh, a parting shot: Does your Master understand the ground-rules for "rants?" It took me some time to realize my male role when a woman is ranting. In fact, I assigned my slave of eight years a signal so I knew only to *listen* and not to offer helpful suggestions to solve her problem. Women don't like men to suggest solutions to rants. Rants are emotional releases; they are not a conversation. It's as jarring to interrupt an emotional scene with logic as it is to interrupt a bottom in subspace by asking them a question requiring thought.

Who are you in relation to what your Master wants

Pretend you have *not* been together for five or ten years. Pretend you've been watching this Master and you're considering petitioning to be their slave. You are at the *interview* stage. You find a casual time to chat, and you ask some questions about what Master is seeking in a slave. Does this Master describe you or somebody else?

Here's the question: Are you still in touch with your Master's wants and dreams? Are you sure? Is it possible Master compromised their dreams for your sake without ever discussing it with you? Might your Master actually be living in the world of "what ifs" and "if onlys?"

I realize this kind of interview probably isn't feasible, but just think for a moment: what have you given up to stay with your Master? What do you think your Master has given up to avoid pissing you off or annoying you to the point of leaving? What is your Master *not* asking you to do because it's either not in your skill set or not something you'd willingly do? I know, I know: you're supposed to be *willing* to do *anything*. But, that is theory; this is reality.

It can be challenging to get two grown-ups to adjust to a Master/slave structure in which you both get your needs met. It can be even more difficult when converting a marriage to an M/s structure. Since this section engages the question of who the slave is in relation to Master, this might be a good time to ask some questions.

Basically, you'll want a written list of Master's expectations of slave's role as much as you'll want a written list of slave's expectations of Master's role. I urge you to do this little exercise. If one of you is not what the other really wants, it's going to be hard to disguise it. As one of you expresses little dissatisfactions, the other person may feel disrespected, unwanted, emotionally distanced, or unloved.

Neither of you are likely to come right out and say: "You are not fulfilling my needs or even my wants. We must radically change what we have been doing or end this relationship."

Neither of you are likely to be willing to step up and confront this particular can of worms unless pushed to the very brink of personal, emotional, or financial survival. Typical reasons include:

- You are too financially entwined; the one wanting to leave can't survive alone.
- You're staying together because you've come to an age at which you don't think there are other M/s partners who could offer you a situation better than your current.
- Your life isn't exactly *bad,* it's just *boring* and unfulfilling.

What to do, what to do?

Unfortunately, there isn't a generalizable answer; the two (or more) of you have to derive this one on your own. However, one of my earlier books is devoted to this specific topic/issue. It's titled: *Master/slave Relations: Solutions 402—Living in Harmony.*

Back to my lead question—what kind of slave does your Master really want, and does their model fit who *you* now are and what *you* now want? If yes, congratulations, it's undoubtedly been a hell of a lot of work. If not, what are you going to do about it?

Relationship durability

Authority-imbalanced relationships share characteristics of vanilla relationships, but they work slightly differently. Here are ten qualities common to long-lasting vanilla relationships. Conventional wisdom tells us these lead to successful marriages.

Open communication
Conventional Wisdom: In casual conversations, those in healthy relationships communicate more than just facts; they communicate emotions and personal reactions to the facts.

My opinion about this situation as it applies to M/s: Masters differ widely about the degree of open communication permitted their slaves. I know one Master who reserves 3-4p on Sunday afternoons to listen to anything slave wishes to say. I know another Master who permits their slave to speak openly once slave has said something like: "Master, permission to speak frankly." Personally, my former slave was not often permitted fully informal "social speech." She could use mid-level speech protocols up to a specific time of day, after which high protocol speech was required until released. I've written extensively about this in other books. Some Masters prefer not to share much information with their slave; other Masters share everything. It rather depends upon the personality of those involved and again raises the question: "Who is this slave in relation to this Master?"

Balance

Conventional Wisdom: Relationships suffer if one person is consistently giving more to the relationship than the other.

My opinion about this situation as it applies to M/s: This condition certainly exists in M/s, but (in my opinion) it's slightly skewed. As I've repeatedly said, while slave is in service to Master, Master is in service to the relationship. Balance is reached in the expression: slave serves Master's wants; Master serves slave's needs.

"Needs," in this sense, are the bottom two levels of Maslow's *Hierarchy of Needs*:
- Level one: Biological and physiological needs: air, food, drink, shelter, warmth, sex, sleep.
- Level two: Safety needs: protection from elements, security, order, law, stability, freedom from fear.

In *Partners in Power,* Jack Rinella's writes: "A slave's power is inversely related to his Master's. Together they create a full sharing of power, the one exercising and holding, the other granting and surrendering."

Chapter 3: slavery

"Bear in mind" Rinella goes on to write: "the 'powerless' partner is such because he or she has surrendered power to the other. This transfer, in fact, makes the one more powerful but at the same time often has, and should have, the effect of empowering each of the participants, not so much disempowering the one but rather changing the focus or type of his or her power. It is a strange dynamic, since it is through surrendering power the submissive partner becomes in fact more empowered."

Compassion

Conventional Wisdom: Compassion is the chief component for friendships. Compassion describes one person's concern and care about the needs of the other person as much as they care for their own needs.

My opinion about this situation as it applies to M/s: Again, my views about how this works in an M/s structure are likely to get me into trouble. So, here it is: Master is responsible for all of slave's needs in order to keep slave in optimal operating order. It is Master's side of the vow to care for all of slave's needs once slave surrenders authority over itself to Master. Thus upon formal collaring, "compassion" is an automatic part of the M/s dynamic.

Honesty

Conventional Wisdom: People in healthy relationships don't hide things from one another. They don't hide liquor bottles and they don't run from topics that make one or both people uncomfortable. Lies undermine trust: trust is the foundation of all long-lasting relationships.

My opinion about this situation as it applies to M/s: No difference. At M/s conferences you hear a great deal about the importance of honesty, integrity, and transparency.

Faithfulness

Conventional Wisdom: Successful couples tough it out when things get rocky in the relationship. Nobody runs away.

My opinion about this situation as it applies to M/s: No difference. For Master or slave to end a relationship is bad enough, but to abandon a relationship is fundamentally opposed to the relationship's core values.

Respect

Conventional Wisdom: People in healthy relationships have learned to respect one another's ideas and opinions.

My opinion about this situation as it applies to M/s: Ongoing respect lies in Master's success in serving the relationship. Respect by slave toward Master would have preceded slave accepting Master's collar. However, there is no uniform commitment for Master to respect slave's ideas and opinions. This point is covered elsewhere in this book.

Conflict Resolution

Conventional Wisdom: Adults in long-lasting relationships have learned how to avoid the *blame game.* They have learned how to prioritize each battle's relative importance and have learned it's okay for partners to have different opinions on topics.

My opinion about this situation as it applies to M/s: Conflict resolution skills are Master's responsibility. It's a leadership skill. At least in my M/s world, slave would not have the authority to initiate conflict resolution tactics. Certainly not overtly, and if done covertly would represent a breach of trust, as slave would be problem-solving at the "relationship" level where slave has no authority. However, as Master Michael adds, "While the slave does not have the authority to initiate conflict resolution tactics, they had better be skilled in (or start learning) the method of conflict resolution that Master uses, or they'll be in for a very rocky ride."

Fun

Conventional Wisdom: Successful long-term couples set aside time to have fun together.

Chapter 3: slavery

My opinion about this situation as it applies to M/s: "Having fun" is the third "rule" in larger BDSM community: 1. Don't hurt your bottom; 2. play within your skill level; 3. have fun. In M/s, Master's determines what is fun: slave, who is pledged to meet Master's *wants* participates as instructed. This can become a touchy topic if Master and slave disagree on what it means to have fun. I can imagine extreme situations where Master's "fun" violates slave's actual needs. This would be the case if a truly sadistic Master thought it fun to cause physical or psychological harm to their slave. This wanders into areas of illegality and is outside the scope of this book. Guidelines for successful relationships differ somewhat in our world from the Land of Vanillas. That's why we're here.

Forgiveness.

Conventional Wisdom: Mature adults realize people make mistakes. So long as the mistakes are not egregious or part of a pattern, and so long as the offender recognizes the action as wrong-headedness and learns from it, forgiveness is a cornerstone of relationship success.

My opinion about this situation as it applies to M/s: This one can be dicey in M/s. "Old school" Masters tended to have the attitude, "the first time you don't do what I ask, it's a mistake and I'll point it out to you. The second time you do it, you disrespect my authority. The third time you do it, you disrespect our relationship and you're dismissed."

My own Master's views "trust" like a fresh piece of copy paper and views "broken trust" like crumpled piece of copy paper. Even though you may try to uncrumple it, it will never again look like a piece of new, unused copy paper. Crumpled paper is heading for the trash.

"Yes," said Master Bert Cutler upon hearing this story at the Butchmann's Experience 2013, "but you can certainly write a beautiful story on a piece of crumpled paper." Thank you, Master Bert. That was a big help.

Within the M/s structure, I personally recommend Masters develop protocols covering not only forgiveness but atonement and release. Those are outside the scope of this book.

Be yourself

Conventional Wisdom: You should like yourself (and your partner should like you) for who you are and not seek to change anything about your individual "style" or personality.

My opinion about this situation as it applies to M/s: I'd assume that the slave likes itself well enough, but if it doesn't, it's slave's responsibility to tell Master. Master is then responsible to help the slave develop greater self-confidence. On the flip side, it's nice if Master likes everything about the slave. However, if there is some aspect of slave that displeases Master, they have the specific authority to require slave to change in any way so ordered. Master's broad authority over the slave distinguishes M/s from D/s or O/p. I realize you may not agree. Remember, none of it matters: it's just how you create your own successful partnership. All I can do is give you ideas to think about.

Alpha and *beta* personalities

I had the privilege to attend Master Stephen's (Stephen_Mar on Fet) fascinating presentation at the GWNN Bash in 2014. He pointed out that one branch of the discussion about *relationship durability* involves recognizing and embracing the role your personality plays within the M/s structure. He offered four distinctions concerning *dominance in slavery:*

- A Master with an *alpha* personality is the "Top Dog." They require total control: this person does everything. They generally aren't interested in suggestions by others.
- A Master with a *beta* personality wants the job done and will delegate it to the most qualified person.
- A slave with an *alpha* personality has an underlying "I can get it done" perspective, but they prefer to "get it done" when in service to someone.
- A slave with a *beta* personality is waiting to be told what to do.

Chapter 3: slavery

As Jen and I were discussing Master Stephen's presentation, she (rather cleverly, in my opinion) noted that while one often finds a *beta* Master partnered with an *alpha* slave in the gay Leather version of M/s, an *alpha* Master is most commonly partnered with a *beta* slave in the heterosexual BDSM version of M/s.

If you're confused, here's a reference point. Master would want a dominant slave for the same reasons a corporate CEO would want a dominant COO (Chief Operations Officer): they get things done.

Master Stephen also discussed the challenge of maintaining the M/s relationship structure when a beta Master is paired with an alpha slave: it can be challenging to get the alpha slave to take instruction. Occasionally my own Master has trouble with me along these lines. She has developed two phrases for pointing out my lapse and bringing me present:
- "boy, how would your last sentence have sounded in protocol?" or,
- "Ah, I see the boy has wandered into its dominant head."

I can take it from there and correct myself.

By the way, according to Master Stephen *discipline* has to be structured differently for a dominant slave than for a submissive slave. Dominant slaves know what they're supposed to do and are used to disciplining those who don't follow *their* orders.

This is all part of the puzzle about how some people who are viewed as dominants in other parts of their lives are to be found in "slave" roles in their private lives. It's also about why their friends and relations think they've joined a cult. Anyway, this may help you to understand your own dynamic and we've included it for that purpose.

Learning to live together

I'll admit to being a self-help program junkie. I can lose hours at a time reading about some way of better managing some aspect of myself nobody really noticed or cared about in the first place. My CEO at work keeps telling me to stop. She says one can't change fundamental aspects of oneself. I'm afraid I disagree. I've been working on myself since I was 26, when I first realized I probably *could* change fundamental aspects of myself. Anyway, I say to myself, unless lots and lots of other people shared my interest in self-help, there wouldn't be this wealth of information and resources.

This brings me to this section's topic: learning to live together (regardless of how long you've been living together).

At "Masters only" workshops during Master/slave conferences questions arise asking how one stays "on" (energized) to keep the relationship fresh after years together. Clearly, there are as many answers as there are people who succeed at it, and the couple's own interpersonal and communication skills determine the results. No silver bullets, I'm afraid. Given all this, here are some examples about how Jen and I work to keep our relationship fresh. You'll have to decide for yourselves whether our approach fits your situation.

Master does not believe you always have to be "on" to remain in M/s head space. While your protocol levels change, *who you are* doesn't change. We've built interaction protocols around general time slots.
- Work time: any time the two of us are engaged on a mutual project. It can be moving furniture, cleaning up the garage, or writing a book. Here, we are more-or-less collegial, except Master makes or approves all final decisions. This is our "default" interaction level: I call her "Master." She calls me whatever comes to her mind at the time. If we're in public, she calls me "Bob," although she knows I find it jarring.
- After arriving home from work but before showering: While still in contact at work by texting, Master lets me know what she wants from our evening together. Sometimes she wants a weeknight to be work time; sometimes she wants social time. We change out of our work clothes immediately upon arriving home. I get into one of three "house uniforms," appropriate for the evening's purpose. Master dresses as she wishes. Often, we'll use a portion of this time to drink a glass of Port or have a cocktail and debrief from our days.

- Evenings: I remind Master of the time if it gets much after seven. Generally, we stop, shower, and get dressed for dinner and for the rest of the evening. We have various levels of dress, but anybody walking in would think either we were doing some kind of dress rehearsal for a play or we're simply nuts. However, once we've showered, our more formal level of protocol remains until we're in bed. (Even our sexual play is wrapped in protocols and ritual. Think "Courtesan" or "Geisha;" it's just more fun for us that way. Purpose, intent, and such, right?)

Understanding anxiety

Anxiety affects Master's quality of leadership and slave's quality of service. Obviously. Anxiety feeds off of many sources: poor self-image, troubles at work, financial problems, sick parents, sick kids, or your own illness. Many things, both little and big, conspire within us to unquiet our minds. Actually, I suspect people (in general) are being affected by anxiety and emotional imbalance far more than they realize. Because anxiety-producing conditions surround us, some portion of M/s relationship disruption undoubtedly results from the background noise of societally-based emotional upset. It's useful to know not all your upsets are caused by your partner.

Here are some numbers and facts for Masters and slaves to consider in the context of their unique relationship.

An October 2011 report from the Centers for Disease Control and Prevention's *National Center for Health Statistics* found 11 percent of Americans over the age of 12 take antidepressants! Astonishingly, about 14 percent took the medication for more than 10 years. That's a hefty number. I won't list all the details, but take a look at research put out by the *Anxiety and Depression Association of America* (ADAA).

- **Generalized Anxiety Disorder** affects 6.8 million adults, or 3.1% of the U.S. population: Women are twice as likely to be affected as men.
- **Panic Disorder** affects 6 million adults, or 2.7% of the U.S. population. Women are twice as likely to be affected as men.
- **Social Anxiety Disorder** affects 15 million people, 6.8% of the population. It is equally common among men and

women, typically beginning around age 13. According to a 2007 ADAA survey, 36% of people with social anxiety disorder report experiencing symptoms for 10 or more years before seeking help.

- **Posttraumatic Stress Disorder** (PTSD) is reported by 7.7 million people: 3.5% of the total population. Women are more likely affected than men. Rape most commonly triggers PTSD: 65% of raped men and 45.9% of raped women develop the disorder. Childhood sexual abuse is a strong predictor of lifetime likelihood for developing PTSD.

Depression aside, let's look at sleep and sleep deprivation. Forty-five percent of Americans say poor or insufficient sleep has affected their activities at least once in the past seven days, (See: National Sleep Foundation's 2013 *Sleep Health Index.)* Four percent of American adults (more than 8.5 million people) used a prescription sleep aid in the month prior to their survey. Use increases with age. In addition, more women (5%) than men (3.1%) over the age of 20 take these drugs, and those with higher education levels are more likely to use them. (See: U.S. Centers for Disease Control and Prevention.)

So, now let's talk about stress and anxiety in the edgy world of M/s relationships. Many believe *illness* is a physical manifestation of your subconscious mental state and attitude. Illness is strongly influenced by *stress.* If illness forces you to bed or to "not be in the mood" for something, this can be interpreted as forced emotional separation: you don't feel well. Some believe relationship stress can produce psychological conditions that manifest as illness. I mention this so either Master or slave can consider the state of their relationship the next time one of you falls ill.

As with most areas of life, some people address identified health problems; others avoid them. Emotional stress can be hard to identify and expensive to treat. As a result, some people ignore signs a professional would catch; others self-medicate. Of course, some people exhibit annoying (but tolerable) behaviors that are not serious enough to require formal treatment. However, some who suspect something to be very wrong with themselves or a loved one consciously dismiss the warning signs. They choose self-delusion and "float the river of de-Nile" as the saying goes. While Master may choose to float such a river; slave doesn't that authority. The slave doesn't have the authority to make decisions about their own physical or mental health: they're obliged to fully disclose medical or psychological concerns to their Master who then decides what to do. As Master is obligated to take care of slave's needs, medical needs rank high on the list.

Remember: you've pledged to be honest and transparent with Master.

But, this isn't a discussion about depression, anxiety or the amount of sleep you're getting. This is a discussion about *trusting your partner* with your health. You may not be as okay (psychologically stable) as you think. It's Master's decision to require you to be checked by a psychologist.

Trusting has multiple facets: not only is slave expected to fully trust Master, but slave is expected to fully trust *itself* to obey Master even when orders appear arbitrary or wrong-headed. More than that, you must trust that in ten or twenty years you will still think your decision to be a slave to this Master was a good idea.

Since conventional wisdom says, *it's always good idea to plan for dragons if one lives in your neighborhood,* here are some ideas for calming a few of the many roots of a slave's anxiety:
- discuss Master's vision of your place in their life in two years;
- plan for times when you bump up against some scary place;
- build protocols enabling you safely to confirm Master understands your concerns;
- if relevant, work through the logistics of polyamory (the issue: cooperation versus competition with a new slave);
- confront your own fear of committing to be your Master's slave, forever;
- accept that whether Master is right or wrong, Master is right; and
- give up the right to do wrong.

This last point came up at a recent conference as I was speaking with a newly established M/s couple. The female Master commented:

"Only then—after he had given up the right to do wrong—could I accept his Petition as my slave." The male slave's comment was: "The thought of never, ever being dishonest in any way is scary. The process of getting there has been very hard. 'Truth' can be so subjective, I anguished about upholding her standards of honesty and the consequences of failure."

Since most of these anxiety-producing fears are rooted in *trust* and *understanding*, solutions center on Master's various abilities. For example, Master must be able to anchor strong trust through consistent wise actions, and establish himself/herself as an empathetic listener with above-average people-management skills.

Tough order, but this level of M/s is not for posers.

Here are some topics. They aren't new topics; however, they are topics Master is going to want to accommodate in some fashion. This is just a sample; individuals have their own unique fears.
- Giving up control over their life…
    o Will Master permit free time? What, even, *is* "free time?"
    o What if I want to go somewhere Master doesn't care about?
    o Will Master support interests he/she doesn't share? (knitting, golf, bowling)
    o Once I surrender authority over myself, how can I get it back without precipitating a financial and emotional crisis? (What are the rules of *dis*engagement?)
    o Believing Master's intentions…
    o This all *sounds* good, but…
        • I don't even trust *myself* to make good decisions, what makes me think Master is better at it than I am? (Alternative: I've been around the block a few times, too, and I have specialized skills/ knowledge greater than Master's.)

I'm fond of one-line summations of complex ideas. I couldn't figure out anywhere else to put them so you're stuck with them grouped here.

- It's not up to the slave to decide whether or not slave is behaving/performing correctly, it's only up to Master. When slave expresses self-doubt, Master may actually interpret what slave is saying as "Master did not choose the correct slave." slave is taking authority away from Master's acceptance of the slave.
- It's slave's responsibility **not** to see certain things Master does. For example, slave would not see Master spill something; slave would simply act to clean it up.
- Over time, slaves learn the difference between being **OF service** to someone and being **IN service** to someone. As a slave *in service,* you are held accountable for the quality and consistency of your service, even when you don't want to serve as you're being asked. In the old days, this was referred to as exhibiting "grace under fire," and included both public and private environments.
- "You don't lose the ability to protect yourself just because you're a slave," as my friend Brett (Fet = LTR) pointed out during one of our 2014 Webinars.
- There is a difference between the autonomy given to slave by Master, and the autonomy required by slave in order to be able to serve Master. (Master Jen: 2014)

Chapter 4: Nuts and Bolts

There are advantages of going to Master/slave conferences all over the U.S.: you get to hear gifted speakers. Slave Caroline is one of those. For years, I've been taking every class I could from her. Some years ago, she commented in her *Leadership Power* workshop: "Leadership is the highest form of service and responsibility for actions related to self and others."

Her sentence turned out to be one of the keys enabling me to understand the concept, "slave is in service to Master, but Master is in service to the relationship." Over the years, I've found some pithy quotes concerning *leadership* by interesting people. I'd like to share them with you. They bear directly on one's leadership role in a Master/slave relationship:

- "Character is power." (Booker T. Washington)
- "Leadership is action, not position." (Donald McGannon)
- "The person who knows HOW has a *job*; the person who knows WHY is the *boss*." (Jim Cathcart)
- "Leadership is the ability to get people to do what they don't want to do and like it." (Harry Truman)
- "Management is doings things right, leadership is doing the right thing. Leadership is all about doing what might not be the best choice but is the right choice." (Peter Drucker)
- "Think like a man of action, act like a man of thought." (Henri Louis Bergson)

Another thing about *leaders:* most have taught themselves to introduce a slight pause as they consider what they are being told. They use the pause to map an appropriate response. There is a formula to it: they hear, they assess what they heard in the context in which it's being said, then they respond. Most people simply *respond* when told something, and then wonder how to fix the little mess they just created.

True leadership is a rare thing. There are many, many facets to leadership and leading. You know this. Here, I'm just going to highlight a few I feel are particularly tricky when it comes to M/s relationships—especially well-established relationships.

Motivators

Some word/actions motivate us to do things; some words/actions motivate us to avoid doing things. As Master, your ability to monitor/control these in yourself and your slave becomes important benchmarks of your success (and the success of your relationship).

Positive motivators

Here are some key points from Daniel Pink's book, *Drive: The Surprising Truth About What Motivates Us*. (Although this is certainly straight from the Land of Vanillas, it provides important perspectives into motivation theory and adapts easily to M/s.)

Autonomy:
Autonomy is a powerful motivator. It's defined as: "the capacity of a rational individual to make an informed, un-coerced decision." Autonomy involves the power to select what you do, the choice of when you do it, the decision of how you do it, and also the choice of who you do it with.

Clearly, these all live in Master's realm and are specifically excluded from the realm of most slaves. However, knowing the components of autonomy and the importance it plays in motivation and self-esteem, Master may wish to consider using the *lack of autonomy* as a training/reinforcing tool.

Translated to M/s: When assigning a task, Master may wish to be particularly clear about the scope of the task, when it is due, and who (if anyone) they are to do it with. Depending upon the task, Master can either direct how it is to be done or ask slave to explain in detail how they intend to approach it.

Hint: when someone with a certain level of knowledge and skill gives an order to someone with a lower (or undefined) level of knowledge and skill, there is room for misunderstanding. There can be hidden assumptions about how best to approach a task. This is an area where Master benefits from being sensitive to their teaching style and their slave's learning style. Master may need to work with slave to verify they both truly understanding the requested task. For example: "Wash the car" has multiple levels of compliance. "Wash the car" does not necessarily mean to remove trash from the car's interior. Similarly, "Wash the car and remove trash from the interior" does not necessarily mean to clean the windows from the inside, etc.

Please don't lose sight of the goal, here: Master is trying to create a positive and supporting (win-win) experience; slave is trying to please Master.

Mastery:
People like to be known as "good" at things: motivation comes from mastering skills and/or knowledge. In M/s, many Masters are motivated by mastering Mastery, itself. Similarly, mastering service and obedience to their Master motivates many slaves. Motivation thrives on passion. This leads to a question: how do you invite passion into your lives? Is each of you someone about whom your partner can be passionate? Personally, Jen and I go to great lengths to remain passionate about one another. We long ago committed to making each night "different" in some way. Sometimes it's the way we dress; sometimes it's the choice of evening activity. Sometimes, it's taking her shopping for shoes or changing our own personal look. Sometimes it's discussing the news; sometimes it's tying out a new sex toy or SM technique.

M/s is about passion, intent, and purpose. Check in: supervise actively. Have fun.

Purpose:

Beyond sex and companionship, you have to think and plan in order to develop a reason (purpose) for your relationship. *Purpose* in a relationship provides the opportunity to achieve something greater than you can on your own. Our sense of worth and importance increases as we see good come from our focused purpose. The topic of *relationship purpose* comes up in many of my conference presentations. I often ask those who have declared a purpose to their relationship to comment whether they think it has made any difference. In general, partners who know which actions support the relationship's greater good report feeling fulfilled and gratified. Of course, I can't tell whether they feel more or less fulfilled and gratified than those who have never given any thought to their relationship, but logic would say the former group is more driven and motivated than those without a clearly unified purpose.

Does all this "motivation stuff" work? Well, when you boil it down, research and common sense about failing relationships focus on one partner's dissatisfaction with how the other partner treats them. Drilling more deeply, the core issue often concerns one partner feeling unrecognized for what they are doing for the relationship's benefit. It's about the same in M/s: When Master recognizes slaves' service in ways the slave feels appreciated, you have a happy slave who works all the harder to please Master.

Negative motivators

Negative motivators reinforce a person's negative self-talk. As negative self-reinforcing phrases actually create our beliefs about ourselves, they lead us into a self-fulfilling loop: we now behave exactly as we were afraid we'd behave. Depending upon how stressed we are, our established thought-patterns replayed throughout our lives with greater or lesser intensity. I'd encourage you to look into "self-talk," for there are very helpful books and resources available.

I discussed "Pathway to Happiness" and also a method of re-programming your mind in the earlier section titled "How do you practice your slavery." If you skipped that section (perhaps because you're not a slave) I'd urge you to go back and read it, for I describe a technique to turn negative self-talk into a positive reinforcing tool.

Negative self-talk affects training, and *training* is central to our lifestyle. The state of a trainee's mind strongly influences how receptive they are to the lesson. Sometimes, the trainee is subconsciously fighting with request/orders. This resistance is born of self-sabotaging negative self-talk we all have experienced. It blocks training efforts. The "loop" is telling them they can't remember the instructions, or they don't agree with the instructions, or you sound like their mother, etc. All this is preventing them from complying with Master's wishes.

If this area interests you, you can look up "Kahler's Drivers" on the Internet. If you'd like to learn more about your own and your partner's motivations, I strongly recommend you take some time and work through this 12-question test: *www.brefigroup.co.uk/acrobat/drivers.pdf*

By way of summarizing, Kahler has identified five thought patterns that shape your thinking—and therefore your life:
- to be perfect;
- to please;
- to try hard;
- to be strong; and
- to hurry up.

Here are some examples of behaviors resulting from negative self-talk based on Kahler's work:
- Fear of the unknown: they are afraid something bad/negative will happen if they do "X."
- Fear of success #1: they *almost* complete a task, but not quite.
- Fear of success #2, work setting: They get the task done, but there's a lot of drama involved and their feeling of success dwindles quickly as they begin to worry they've left things out.
- Procrastination: they say such things as, "Once I clean up my desk…" or "Once I'm financially stable…"
- Locked inside their own box: "I always have trouble at parties," or "I always feel that people are judging me," or "I can never get this right."

To some extent we all have thoughts like this, but getting stuck in such loops can contaminate our lives in bad ways. For those of us in our M/s world, it's useful for Master to know this is a potential trouble spot when it comes to guiding the slave.

By the way, some of the questions therapists (or you) can ask to break up this kind of thinking include:

- Who says you must be perfect (etc.)?
- What is *enough*? Who says how much is *enough*?
- What will happen if you do not do "X?" What bad things will happen? What good things will happen?

Behavioral motivators are well researched and there is a LOT of material available about them. I encourage you to explore.

However…

Don't lose sight of this: "Where there is kindness there is goodness and where there is goodness there is magic." (Cinderella, 2015 Version)

Leadership

Thinking about leadership

> "Leadership first, management second.
>
> No management success can compensate for leadership failure."
>
> —Stephen Covey,
> *7 Habits of Highly Effective People*

In keeping with the slightly off-kilter writing style I use, I want to spend just a few minutes exposing you to ways of shifting your thinking about leadership.

To set this up, I'll give you some really good "tried-and-true" quotes about traditional leadership that apply equally to the business world or to relationships.

- Vision without action is a daydream. Action without vision is a nightmare. [Japanese proverb]
- Leadership is the capacity to translate vision into reality. [Warren Bennis]
- People ask the difference between a leader and a boss. The leader leads and the boss drives. [Theodore Roosevelt]
- One of the tests of leadership is the ability to recognize a problem before it becomes an emergency. [Arnold Galsgow]
- Predicting the future is easy. It's trying to figure out what's going on now that's hard. [Fritz R. S. Dressler]

Now, a different way to slice that watermelon…

Methods of leading

Leading by inquiry: Learn how great leaders manage meetings (and people) by asking questions. Here are some book titles to consider:

- *Change Your Questions, Change Your Life: 10 Powerful Tools for Life and Work* by Marilee Adams. (Virtually everything we think and do is generated by questions. Adams shows readers how to consistently choose the questions that can lead them to success, both personally and professionally.)
- *Leading with Questions: How Leaders Find the Right Solutions by Knowing What to Ask* by Michael J. Marquardt. (Previously described.)
- *A More Beautiful Question: The Power of Inquiry to Spark Breakthrough Ideas* by Warren Berger. (Questioning—deeply, imaginatively, "beautifully"—can help us identify and solve problems, come up with game-changing ideas, and pursue fresh opportunities. Berger teaches you how to master the art of inquiry and raise questions no one else is asking in order to uncover powerful answers.)

Chapter 4: Nuts and Bolts

Leading by example: If you expect your follower to do something in a particular way, not only must you demonstrate the action you want followed, you have to be clear that you then expect *them* to change their behavior to conform to your lead. If you want your slave to detail your car, demonstrate the expected level of detailing. If you want your slave to serve you in a particular manner, demonstrate that service and discuss the details overtly. My former Mistress would sometimes behave in a certain way, expecting that I would emulate her. However, without a specific directive, I usually missed the point that she intended me to change my behavior to match hers. I can be a little dense.

Leading by changing directions: Okay, you're in a rut. You've tried a few different leadership styles and nothing seems to produce your desired results. Two quips come to mind:
- "If you find yourself in a hole, the first thing to do is stop digging" (Will Rogers).
- "Insanity: doing the same thing over and over again and expecting different results" (Albert Einstein).

So: change gears. Declare that your relationship is going to take on a new (radical?) project. Commit yourself to your Community (whatever that looks like to you).

Like leading by example, moving in a different direction and changing things up is Master's decision: it simply does not require discussion. A decision to radically change some aspect of your relationship is an issue of visionary leadership. Ah, and to answer the niggling concern your slave/friends/community may think you're nuts, I offer you this one: "The distance between insanity and genius is measured by success" (Ian Fleming).

Leading with active listening: *Listening* is only half of the communication equation: successful listeners have developed the skill of listening *actively*—they summarize what the other person says and repeat it to verify they heard it correctly. If you're listening without reflecting what you're hearing, you might as well be a stone. Well, not quite that bad, but less than great.

By the way, this *reflection* does not involve analysis. The concept comes from the world of Neuro-Linguistic Programming (NLP) called "mirroring and matching," and its purpose is to give the other person a window into your understanding of what they are saying. In our nuanced world of M/s, what one person thinks they said may not at all be what the other person heard them say. As the great writer Russell Hoban famously said, "When you come right down to it, how many people speak the same language even when they speak the same language?"

Resources in this area include my own book, *Master/slave Relations: Communications 401—the advanced course,* and any book or course that will expose you to Neuro-Linguistic Programming (NLP) communication methods. You might try an Amazon or Barnes and Noble search for "NLP Books."

Living authentically

This is a tough section to write. It doesn't apply to all readers; it applies to readers who react negatively to what you're about to read. If this section makes enormous sense to you, it is probably not relevant because you've already realized this and learned how to live in authenticity. However, for those for whom this section hits home, your "monkey brain" is likely to shift into "defense mode" as you object to what I write. I'm not going to go into much detail; if you're interested in this topic, you will probably want to do additional research. Or not; I'm not your parent.

In summary, the issue is this: *having spent your life trying to modify your likes and dislikes in order to fit in with and to be accepted by others, you have lost the ability to distinguish between what you really do enjoy and what you think you **should** enjoy.*

Sages throughout time have railed at us, "To thine own self be true." We know this. However, we also know these sages have been evasive about how to identify what is honest and true for ourselves. We're admonished to follow our hearts; we're not told how to know what our hearts want. *Others* (including social media) tell us we should want, and they tell us so often and forcefully we usually give in and go along with it.

Chapter 4: Nuts and Bolts

We go along with it because we are drawn to seek social approval. We want to fit in, at least to a reasonable extent. Worse yet, even when we realize we are not acting authentically and don't really believe in what we are saying or doing, we continue anyway. Often, we consciously "act as if" we believe in what we are doing for fear our family, friends, or community won't approve of us. Even in cases where we realize our publicly stated ideals, goals, and objectives are really beyond our capabilities, we continue to go through the same loops; we continue to defend our public face based upon some (made up) fear that others (undefined) will think less of us. We hide our perceived shortcomings, or we pretend they don't exist. In doing so, we unwittingly add another layer of inauthenticity to those layers already built up.

Personal satisfaction flows from mental, emotional, and behavioral congruity. This describes a person whose actions reflect correct thinking; correct thinking ties to what Stephen Covey refers to as *character ethic.* Taking this one step further, personal happiness generally flows from someone who is internally aligned: in-authenticity breeds emotional discomfort.

It's hard to be happy with yourself once you realize you're public face differs from your own self-assessment. Of course, it's not as though you're doing this with full consciousness; some of your behavior is culture-driven (keeping up with the Jones's), and some are driven by a need to be accepted by those whom you think matter. Most people tolerate a little difference between the way they know they should behave and the way they actually behave. This is rather automatic. It's easier than admitting your behavior could do with some polishing and then starting down the more challenging path of taking conscious control of your unconscious actions. Every time we take the path of "looking good" or "avoiding looking bad" rather than walking the path that projects who we are or would like to become, inauthenticity creeps in compromises our authentic selves.

Unfortunately, habits compromising our wants, needs, and beliefs developed when we were quite young. When we spoke our version of "the truth" as children, adults usually made it clear we were wrong. Adults didn't just tell us we were young and exploring with our ideas, they often told us we were wrong in our thinking and (perhaps) in our actions.

Once we began to compromise who we thought we were in order to project back to adults the child they wanted to see, we were already well along on a path of habituation that becomes more and more difficult to alter as we, ourselves, grow up. For imagery, think of each misdirection by someone (whether a parent, other adult, or other child) as a little pebble thrown into a calm pond. It makes a ripple. Each pebble makes a ripple. After a while, you conclude that all ponds have ripples. Many adults spend years and years trying again to find a pond with the unbroken surface: it's called *enlightenment.*

However, for most of us--for those of us who have not yet reached what some call *enlightenment*--it becomes more and more difficult to know who we are when our internal guidance system (our internal knowledge of what is right and wrong for us individually) is repeatedly compromised in large and small ways. We deny this to ourselves and to others, of course. Sometimes we deny our own falseness quite vocally. As Ralph Waldo Emerson once remarked to someone who had engaged him in argument: "What you are thunders so loud that I cannot hear what you say to the contrary."

As an adult, when we lost sight of *who we are at our core,* there's really no starting point to regain our perspective. We must first recognize the state we're in and develop the motivation to change. At this point, it's all a matter of personal willpower. It's a matter of consciously fighting our "monkey brain" (reactive self), redefining our values and reconstructing ourselves as we know we wish to be.

Unfortunately, when our monkey brain wakes up and realizes your messing around in territory it's used to controlling, it goes into high alert. In a soft, cajoling voice it says to you: "Don't be silly. Behavior is determined by our inherent character, our circumstances, and our upbringing. Leave yourself alone, you've done okay 'till now. But in our hearts, we know our monkey brain is lying to us. In our heart of hearts, we really know we, ourselves, determine our own actions moment by moment through the exercise of our own will. We also know that to exercise personal will in this way, we must take responsibility for every word we speak and every gesture we make.

And that's a truly challenging task.

Which is why it's so challenging to live in authenticity.

Control

Master Arach has phrased this core concept so concisely that I can't impove upon it: "Control is something you take: authority is something you give. Control is action, authority is the right to take that action."

Know what Master can and cannot control...

"Master commands the ship but cannot control the weather or the seas." (I can't remember where I heard this, so if you know the source, please contact me.) As Master, your challenge is to know what you can and cannot control and to act responsibly in both areas. For example, while you can't control the consequences of your actions and you can't command happiness, you *can* control the environment that introduces *thoughtfulness* to your actions in order to enable *happiness* to thrive.

> "The desires of a Master should outweigh the desires of a slave
>
> but the needs of a slave should not outweigh the desires of a Master."
>
> —Jack McGeorge

I've found the following concepts to be helpful over the years...

Master can control *honor* and *integrity*. If you can successfully repeat some action, you're consistent. Your moral character depends upon acting consistently with respect to your personal code of ethics. Reliability is derived from consistency, and consistency builds trust. Honor and integrity are also linked to reliability: they all depend upon consistency.

Tough decisions, decisions based on ethical principles, may not be in your own best interest, but are the "right thing to do" in terms of fairness, honesty, and integrity. When someone fails to make consistently ethical decisions, they are said to have *situational ethics* and they are seen as being "out of integrity," inconsistent, and untrustworthy. That's a problem.

Master can make instructions clear. Avoid "mush words." *Mush words* are words open to subjective interpretation. "boy/girl, bring my stuff from the car." "Stuff?" What will you do (how will you react) when the retrieved "stuff" did not include what you had wanted?

Let's ratchet this up a level: "slave, pack up our toy bag; we're leaving for the party in 20 minutes." What does *that* mean? What goes in the toy bag? How is slave expected to know all the equipment to pack? Isn't this something like picking up a high-end digital camera (your property, just like your slave) and, after turning it on, simply clicking the shutter without framing your shot (defining your target)? You'd get a picture (the filled toy bag), but it's a crap shoot whether or not everything you wish is in there.

M/s is about *command and control.* This means you have to be specific about your command and then monitor its execution by way of expressing control. By the way, that's why written protocols are so important—they force you to be clear about what you want.

Master can avoid "surprises." While Master makes the final decision, successful leaders gather a lot of relevant information before announcing decisions affecting key staff. Unless Master is used to leading teams in a work setting, it can be a challenge to remember that while Master knows what Master knows, slave may have a different "take" on what Master thinks they know. Master ignores slave (or fails to probe what slave knows about the topic) at the relationship's peril. Master can get away with unilateral decisions in some areas, but not so well in other areas. There will be consequences if slave believes Master makes unilateral decisions in conflict with the slave's best interests. Message: Take time to plan *with* your partner. Learn to set your viewpoint aside while listening actively for information you may not have.

Master can connect daily. Connecting emotionally with another person can be *really* tricky. For starters, you both must agree what you mean by "connection." Additionally, you'll want to know how you each take in information (auditory, kinesthetic, visual, gustatory, olfactory) and your respective "love languages" (words of affirmation, acts of service, receiving gifts, quality time, physical touch). For example, while "connection" for one person may involve doing something cerebral. "connection" for someone else may concern eye contact and quality of conversation.

Master can create opportunities for control and for obedience. This is not a vanilla relationship. This takes thought and creative action. If you try to drift through an M/s relationship, it will sooner-or-later disintegrate. While Master certainly *could* do Tasks A, B, and C, assigning them to the slave *and following up and recognizing slave for completing the tasks correctly* reinforces your command and control. Master gets to feel Masterful and slave gets to feel satisfaction. In my world, *satisfaction* is a necessary condition leading to *happiness.*

> Master should be the source of all good things by way of fostering addiction.
>
> —Brett (Fet = LTD)

Know what you're looking for

When my relationship with Jen started, we weren't a particularly good fit. In some areas, we were spectacular; in others, we were in direct conflict. None of Jen's close friends were rooting for me and none of my close friends were rooting for her. We had a lot of clashes, many quite visible to casual friends. One time, as we were working through our ongoing crises, we sat down and wrote out the *Top Ten Things We Wanted In A Partner.*

Jen took a lot of care preparing her list; it took her a couple of weeks. I had an easier time of it. I had only six points. As Jen looked through her list, she commented that she felt I fulfilled the bottom eight of her "10 wants" but not the top eight. This was fairly sobering, for there were now three spinoff questions:

- Would she compromise and agree to live without her top two wants? (Not likely.)
- Would I be able to change some of my core beliefs and behaviors enough to fill her top two wants? (Possibly but not obviously, as one of her points opposed one of my own core values.)
- Would the awareness I was not her perfect match either:
    - be counterbalanced by what I *could* offer her, or
    - slowly kill our relationship.

I related this story to give you a context for the concluding point: not all needs are created equal. Whether you're thinking of kink needs or emotional needs, some are 10-pounders and some are 6-pounders. At the extremes, Master has the ethical requirement to step aside from a relationship where they know they can't meet their slave's primary needs. Likewise, slave has the matching obligation to step aside if they believe they cannot meet their Master's primary wants.

So: what's in *your* wallet? How is your relationship weathering the years?

Wants can change over time. What one person wants in another can change over time. Obviously, that presents a question: what are your options if one of you concludes you really want a partner with substantially different skills or knowledge? End the relationship? Compromise? Retrain Master to want you? Retrain slave to provide the desired service? Add another person to the relationship to bring back the spark?

> If you wait for life, you will find life also waits for you. In order to lead an exciting life, you have to be excited. You also have to lead.

Answers depend on circumstances, of course, but discussions at this level of dissatisfaction are bound to be emotionally upsetting. That's the point. If you're only now discovering you don't really want what you have, there will be some talking to do. In my experience, emotional discussions benefit from starting by agreeing neither of you will intentionally wound the other person emotionally. Communication pays off, knowing your own and your partner's needs pays off, and commitment to resolve your issues pays off.

Perspective

I have placed some techniques throughout this book to provide some perspective to life in an M/s household. This one is for Masters who are feeling burned out from making all the large and small relationship decisions. *Decision exhaustion* tends to show up during a relationship's early years; over time, Master usually works out ways to deal with it. However, there is an exception: an unhappy slave may express passive-aggressive hostility by asking Master to make or reconfirm virtually every decision. While this may be slave's way of alerting Master that the slave is done with the relationship, such behavior is a disservice to the relationship and can lead to reciprocal anger. In case this is an issue for you, I'll go over the general concept.

Some orders are Big Orders; some orders are little orders. Some situations involve Life Decisions, some decisions simply involve where to eat dinner. "It's important for Masters to steward their energy," says my friend Brett (Fet = LTR). As leaders, Masters are susceptible to decision exhaustion. A symptom: saying "whatever" or "I don't care." Consider developing a protocol requiring slave to bring three options when asking for your choice on some issue. Remember, too: a stressed Master can say, "Not now, slave; I need an hour of downtime."

If slave wishes to bring up a topic potentially leading to an emotional interchange, consider asking yourself:
- Who cares about the outcome? Why do they care?
- Does this issue affect the relationship? If so, how, why, how strongly?
- Will you remember this issue or topic in five years? One year? One month?

Sometimes a decision's importance becomes skewed because one or the other of you is attached to the outcome. A particularly thoughtful Master (who also practices Buddhism) once told me that people can have trouble *doing the right thing* to the degree they care about (are attached to) the outcome. A Master who focuses on the *results* of slave's performance (versus the *intent* of slave's actions) must forever be disappointed; no slave will succeed in aligning their lives with such a Master.

By the way—the prior paragraph carries broader implications: it suggests you're not going to be able to establish an honest M/s dynamic to the extent you care what your partner thinks of you—and *vice versa*. You both must feel free to speak without concern over repercussions from saying the Truth. Theory, right?

Here are some other potentially complicating factors that could affect Master's ability to maintain an impartial perspective about their slave. Some of these are controversial: they are simply viewpoints I've heard bandied about from time to time.

- Having a sexual relationship with your slave may compromise Master's ability to give clean orders because Master is too emotionally involved with the person.
- Moving in with slave who contributes funds to maintain the house may compromise Master's decision-making abilities. (This is a derivative of: "He who has the gold, rules." Master may not feel comfortable requiring slave to make personal changes against their will for fear the slave would choose to leave the relationship rather than comply.)
- It's hard to make fundamental changes when you live within a set of nearly invisible social and cultural norms: you can't see your own bonds. (This is exemplified in the movie, "Matrix.")

Most decisions are compromises, and I'm certainly not proposing anyone give up sex or financial support for the sake of maintaining greater impartiality. I'm just pointing out some of the complexities of M/s structures that tend to be carefully ignored.

Moving right along, emotional upsets can distort your perspective. Perhaps one of the harder lessons for Master to master is to "let the storm storm around you and not become you" as Master Obsidian commented at a recent MAsT meeting. This brings us neatly to the next topic.

Emotions

Temper gets you into trouble. Pride keeps you there. [*Leadership* vol. F no. 11]

"Being Upset" versus "Having an Upset"

In 1975, I went through a training course called *est*. That stood for *Erhard Seminars Training,* and it still exists as *The Landmark Education Forum.* There, I learned a distinction that's had a profound impact on my life. They made the distinction between "being upset" and "having an upset." Their point was, the phrase "I am upset" describes (and reinforces) your emotional state of being upset: by stating you are upset, you are declaring that you are not fully in control of yourself.

Worse, you're now *at the effect* of being upset; your emotions have run off with you. In a sense, your rational self has been hijacked. There are consequences for losing control of your emotional self. The person toward whom you are upset or angry can use the opportunity to manipulate you because you're being controlled by your emotions. This is not a good position to be in. If it's Master who is upset, you now have a disarmed Master.

All of our anger and frustration is self-induced. The world might invite us to be upset, but we choose to accept the invitation.

—Sue Fitzmaurice

Stopping an upset

To avoid having a disarmed Master, you can teach yourself to do *pattern interrupts*. This is a concept from NLP (Neuro-Linguistic Programming) and discussed extensively in most Tony Robbins self-empowerment programs. The moment you sense you are getting angry, change your (emotional) state. Stand up. Sit down. Stretch. Take three deep breaths. Go get a drink of water. *DO* something different than you've been doing. Change your physical position as a way of buying time to get control over your emotional state. If you can stop the process of becoming angry and get control of yourself, you can then learn to **choose** your reaction. This isn't an overnight fix, but it suggests a path for gaining better self-control.

To help you choose your reaction, think about how you can be the cause of your reaction, rather than being at the effect of your anger. Translation: Choose to *have an upset*. This is something like choosing to *have* an ice cream cone. In the same way you can choose to have a chocolate or vanilla ice cream cone, you can learn to choose whether you will or will NOT have an upset. (Hint: Just before you're about to explode, you will sense some physical sensation in your body. In my own case, the back of my scalp starts to tingle. This provides only a second or two to act to change my response to my triggered reaction. However, a second or two is **plenty** of time to change your emotional state.)

You are going to have to make up your own method of breaking the action-reaction cycle to turn it into an action-action cycle. Ultimately, you are responsible both for your actions and reactions. This applies equally to your slave.

Master your state and you'll sharply reduce the unexpected explosions and upsets common to every relationship. Ask yourself: why are you even bothering with this upset? What's your

> A suggestion: Recognize upsets in order to stop them
>
> Make a pact with your partner: both of you agree to recognize when one or both of you are *choosing* to have an upset, rather than *being* upset.
>
> This helps reinforce each of you for making this change from the way you've previously handled unsettling situations.

motivation? Do you want the problem to stop recurring or do you only want to stop the person from being upset?

Chapter 4: Nuts and Bolts

Causes of upsets

Nope, I'm not a psychologist, but I've gone through a lot of personal therapy and reading in an effort to get better control of myself. So: what do you think causes most upsets? Actually, it's a pretty concise list:

- Once upon a time something happened. You were embarrassed. You were offended. You resented it. However, you couldn't do anything about it. Now, when similar issues arise, you react by being upset. When you feel you are more distressed than you think you should be under these conditions, chances are you've just landed on top of your emotional baggage. The remedy is to let go of the trigger; let go of the situation causing you to relive the upset. Unfortunately, it may take a good deal of therapy to identify the root cause.

- *Homo Sapiens*, as wild creatures, had to watch out for threatening situations. Among modern-day Americans, this bias towards caution can lead us to be suspicious and emotionally closed to unknown experiences, whether it's tasting a new food or meeting people not quite like us. You can gain greater control over your own reactions to new people and situations by adopting more of an observer view. Enforce detachment. For readers who want to go further down this path, it's the path of forgiveness and patience laced with the practice of daily gratitude.

- Some people nourish their upsets and resentments daily. They've made them into lifelong friends. They wouldn't know quite how to go through the day if they weren't constantly bitching about something. For those of you who listen to *Prairie Home Companion*, the way Garrison Keillor's "mother" speaks to him provides a great example. If he says something is good, she finds ways to show it's not good at all. In fact, it's really bad. If he doesn't call her as often as she wishes, she heaps buckets of shame and mortification on him. Unhappiness is her life. My father's mother was like that.

In my experience, it's possible to convert bumpy upsets into more even fields by learning to disengage emotionally and to view the occurrence (whatever it is) as a one-off "phenomenon." Stop feeding it with your personal story: destroy the loop that says once "A" is triggered, B, C,

D, E, F, and G have to follow.
They don't have to follow; you're letting them follow. Stop it!

Tom Miller's audio CD program *Self-Discipline and Emotional Control* can help you learn how to stop your runaway emotions.

Managing upsets with compassion

Okay: one or the other of you experienced strong emotional reactions to something. You blew up. It wasn't trivial or the exploding person wouldn't have risked revealing that side of themselves. It's tough to quickly regain composure to manage such a situation with grace. One option, of course, is to call Grace. Grace usually likes to be welcomed with gratitude. While you're sitting in your warm apartment or home having an emotional meltdown, consider where you are, really. It can help your sense of perspective.

Really, you're in the United States. You have adequate housing and food, you're safe from predators, there is a good healthcare system, and you are probably earning money at a job. Statistically, you're in a very small percentage of the world population. According to the United Nations Development Programme's "Human Development Report" of July, 2014, fully 50% of the world's population live on less than $2.50 per day, and 80% live on less than $10 a day. 22,000 children die daily as a direct result of poverty. Something like 1.1 billion people have inadequate access to water. It's pretty sobering. Next time you or your partner hit an emotional landmine, you might reflect on this and hug one another and go out for a cup of coffee.

Once you've learned methods for converting upsets from an emotional to a thinking state, there are some strategies Master can use to improve the overall outcome.
* Recognize and honor their emotional reaction. (*e.g.,* "I understand X has upset you.").
* Express compassion instead of judgment. Express understanding; show appreciation instead of criticism. (*e.g.,* "I see now how this has upset you and I appreciate you're

willingness to express your emotions in front of me.").
- Demonstrate willingness to change instead of blaming them. (*e.g.*, "I apologize if something I said triggered you; can we talk about this and learn from it?").
- Offer reassurance instead of shame. (*e.g.*, "Know that I cherish you and we can work out ways so this does not happen again.").
- Express acceptance instead of guilt. (Most emotional outbursts result from the perception of a breach of trust. Masters usually learn to accept the message(s) hidden in upsets and use them in a positive way. However, to the extent **Master** becomes reactive in this setting and says hurtful things that make slave feel guilty, the relationship will be wounded.)
- Demonstrate curiosity instead of making them wrong. (*e.g.*, "What just happened? What's led up to this upset?" Great leaders lead with questions.).

Recognize that upsets generate false memories

Like historians and novelists, we construe our own histories as we see them. Our version of past events creates our reality. Here's how it works. Something happens. We simultaneously assess and interpret what happened. We assign meaning to the event, categorize its importance, and draw conclusions. We identify what we will do and what we will not do about the event. We then form lingering opinions. This melding (or collapse) between *what happened* and *the meaning we assign to it* occurs in an instant. Objective memory of what "really" happened disappears in a flash, and we're left only with our reconstruction of what happened as seen through the filters of our lives.

The thing of it is, what objectively happened and how we subjectively remember what happened are two independent and separate occurrences. Our subjective version of whatever happened becomes the stuff and story of our lives. We can spice up or water down our stories. We tell the long or short version; we add drama or subtlety. The kind of story you tell depends upon your archetype. Warriors tell stories of aggression and battle; victims tell stories of being used. Regardless of how clever we are or how different we believe the circumstances to be, what continually emerges is pretty much what we've previously experienced: we're in a loop. While we might believe our stories are new, it usually turns out there are only two or three basic themes repeatedly playing themselves out, often in ingenious ways.

Our stories represent the richness of what it means to be human. There is a power, validity, and value in them. However, you'll want to keep your background stories from spoiling your present life. This brings us to what we might call the downside of stories: our interpretations keep us stuck. Without thought, we overlay our stories on current events and put a spin on almost everything that happens to us.

It may help to break such loops when you realize the stories we tell are only our interpretation of events and are no more true or false than another interpretation.

I don't want to keep going along these lines, for this is not a philosophy/psychology book.

If you're interested in exploring ways of interrupting your reactive/revisionist actions after upsets, I (for the third time) recommend Tom Miller's audio course: *Self-Discipline and Emotional Control.* Here is a four-line summary of what he teaches you to understand and to control:

- emotions are always real;
- they come from your horse (often called your "monkey brain");
- but, they are not your emotions;
- it's what your horse has created as the reason things are done a certain way.

Miller's material is about the: "When you did X, I feel Y because I made it mean Z" loop. This is an extremely powerful course and not for the faint of heart. He uses strong language: actually, he yells at you. As he points out, that's about the only way to get through to your horse (monkey brain).

Difficulties

The word "difficulty" is a "mush word." It means different things to different people in different situations. If someone says they're "having a difficult time" or "in a difficulty," we can guess about their problems, but we don't really know what they mean unless they offer explanations. Furthermore, expressions such as "having difficulties" or "having problems" is a code meaning they're not happy with their emotional condition but don't really want to talk about it.

Additionally, *difficulties* have different causes and different solutions depending on their nature and your nature. A *difficulty* prompting one person to work harder may cause another person to have an emotional breakdown.

I'm bringing up this concept because what appears difficult for one person may be easy for another. Master may make an assignment they consider pretty straightforward but slave views as *daunting*. This section is meant to help demystify the concept of "difficult."

Luck Difficulty versus Effort Difficulty

The first distinction is whether the difficulty is related to *effort*. If something is difficult but the outcome doesn't depend much on effort, then it must depend on luck. If you're having a difficult time putting a jigsaw puzzle together, there's not much you can do about it beyond sticking with it and looking harder for the correct shapes.

Luck difficulty and *effort* difficulty are often confused. Publishing a profitable book is difficult, but it's mostly effort difficulty. If you stick at it and continue to hone your writing and marketing skills, experience shows you're likely to succeed. It's about the same for learning a new language. Success is really determined by the amount of time you commit to the project.

Varieties of Luck

There are different kinds of "luck difficulty." Some luck happens only once: your physical size enables you to excel in some activity or sport, or you're born with some genetic gift and find yourself composing symphonies by age 5 like Mozart. Other types of luck continue over time. As you gain excellence in a field, luck may have been involved early in the process but become unnecessary. For example, you may find yourself at the right place at the right time with the right training. Voila! You're in luck. Benefits and rewards will follow you once you begin to gain recognition for your expert knowledge and skills. In situations where greater expertise pays greater rewards, the requirement for *luck* gives way to the requirement for *tenacity* (another word for *effort*).

Quantifying Difficulty

The setting: Master has given slave an assignment the slave views as somewhat difficult.

Difficult assignments can be made easier by breaking them down into their component parts and putting parameters around each part. It helps to write out all the steps. Once slave sees the actual scope of work, it builds self-confidence about starting the task. It also makes the task appear less formidable. In the world of business, these are called "project management sheets" or "time-and-task sheets" or "milestone analyses." You can build protocols to manage projects. Here are some of the more common headings I used with my own slave to manage projects (remember: I have Asperger Syndrome.)

- What is to be accomplished, who is going to do it, when it is to be done?
- Who wants this project completed and why do they want it? (Sub-question: what if it either does not get accomplished as planned or is accomplished incorrectly?)
- What resources are required to complete this task: time, money, training?
- What are everyone's roles and responsibilities? (This is relevant even if only Master and slave are working on the project; it avoids confusion stemming from false assumptions of responsibility.)
- Where are we likely to need outside (specialized) assistance?
- What are the "critical failure points" of this project and possible unintended consequences?
- How long will each phase of this project take to complete and what are the consequences for later phases of not completing a preceding phase on time?
- At what stages should we insert a "project review and feedback" loop?
- At what points should the slave check back with Master with status-updates?
- How—what form or format—should the slave use for these updates?
- Ultimately, what are the "conditions of satisfaction" Master

expects to see to agree the task was well done?

Larger (longer-term) difficult tasks involve different questions depending upon the type of difficulty you're encountering. For example, if you're taking on a challenge such as "working on your Mastery (or slavery)" you'll need to outline a plan of attack able to sustain you for years. By the way, you can't treat all difficult tasks the same way. Some demanding tasks require acceptance while others require aggression; some require responsiveness while others require stoicism. Knowing the kind difficulty you are facing makes a lot of difference.

Anyway, here are a few words on various approaches to difficult tasks.

- If the difficulty involves one-time luck, then you're either in luck or not in luck. Win/lose.
- If the difficulty is not a one-time affair, then you have to decide how much work it will take to accomplish the task without luck already on your side.
- If the difficulty involves both luck and skill and is to be a repeated experience (such as playing the stock market with a "system"), you must put yourself in a position to be lucky. Using the stock or commodities markets as examples, "putting yourself in a position to be lucky" involves such things as *loss tolerance, risk management,* and *patience.* If the system actually works, you have to be able to steel yourself against consecutive losing strings because those will only be noise. Regardless of the endeavor, you will have to account for the possibility your luck may end tomorrow, or it might not. You have to be prepared to be adaptable; you have to be prepared to tolerate ambiguity. (I used to run a commodity futures trading company, in case you wondered about this paragraph.)
- If the difficulty concerns in-depth mastery of a skill or a field of study, then buckle down and get aggressive. Find someone who has been successful in this field and model yourself after them: find a coach. Rewards tend to correlate to the number of study hours you put in. As I've mentioned elsewhere in this book, "mastery" is defined as focused study/practice in excess of 10,000 hours.
- If the difficulty involves mastering a wide breadth of information to perform a task at a certain level of proficiency, be patient and focus on small gains. Celebrate little improvements. Embrace

boredom and build habits that stay the same for years.

Punishment, correction, resolution, and atonement

There are many viewpoints about *punishment* in the M/s community. The best I can do is make bullet points of some of the more prominent perspectives. For these points, "transgressions" mean the slave has not done as asked, however slave was not willfully opposing Master.

- *Punishments for transgressions are part of the relationship.* The very idea D-types punish s-types for slight transgressions comes from the world of heterosexual BDSM fiction. It further fuels the public view of authority-imbalanced relationships as anchored in abuse. Masters who punish minor transgressions seem to view the slave as property whom they may treat however they wish.
- *Transgressions represent a non-alignment of slave to Master's will: we need to discuss it.* The s-type in a formal M/s relationship has sworn to serve and to obey. The slave has pledged to align itself with Master's will. It can be challenging for one person always to know the will of another: missteps happen.
- *Transgressions represent Master's failure to adequately train the slave."* Since the slave in an M/s dynamic is so highly motivated to please Master through service and obedience, any failures in these areas rests solidly at Master's feet. Master has failed to properly train and/or control the slave.

The entire "punishment" discussion is a diversion. There's no need to have to punish a slave; simply require obedience. So long as they obey, then there really isn't a problem, is there? This dovetails neatly with the theory that if the slave disobeys, clearly the idea Master has "total power" is inappropriate. If nothing else, Master obviously didn't have the power to compel the slave to obey without punishment.

Some background

I suspect quite a bit of friction within an M/s dynamic occurs because Master doesn't discern the difference between *reactance* and *resistance*.

Chapter 4: Nuts and Bolts

Reactance vs. Resistance

Reactance is a response to being surprised about something; resistance is willful disobedience.

Reactance represents your unguarded emotional response to an unanticipated event. One can react to good or to bad news or events. Reactance commonly occurs when your safety or authority are challenged. As Master makes all the significant decisions, sooner or later, the slave is bound to react to a decision or two.

Reactance looks like this: You give an order; your slave reacts to the order by…
- Looking at you with defiance,
- Showing an expression of exasperation or disgust,
- Rolling their eyes or replying in a way that questions the order, itself.

Reactance occurs with all couples and in all work settings. It's nothing unusual. Perhaps the most common low-level irritant occurs when the slave reacts with some vanilla-sounding reply such as: "Oh, sure. I'll go get it."

When this happened with my prior slave, my usual reaction was to ask: "And how would *that* sound in protocol?" This was generally enough to get my slave to recognize the lapse and to restate the sentence as: "Yes, Master, I'll go get it." In my current slave role, I get the message when Master says: "boy?!" in her particular Tone of Voice.

Let me step up the scale a little bit. The time will come when Master issues an order and the slave reacts to it in a way you feel must be addressed. Failure to address the issue risks degrading the nature of the authority-exchange upon which the relationship is based.

In such cases, I recommend you consider changing your emotional state. Stop the conversation and change your own and your slave's physical positions. For example, stop speaking, turn your body to face your slave directly and simply ask: "slave, what just happened, here?"

Unless this episode triggered an emotional outburst on one of your parts, this is a time for the slave to *refocus* and discuss the underlying cause of the reactance. A Master with an open mind and open heart will learn a great deal at this point—often about himself/herself rather than about the slave. (Note to Masters: This is a time you get to assess your degree of mastery over yourself and your own emotions.)

Reactance unaddressed is likely at some point to become *resistance*.

Resistance occurs when the submissive/slave opposes Master's dominance, whether unconsciously or purposefully. Now, you've got a challenge. Directly opposing Master's authority is a strong signal something fundamental is amiss. This requires some careful probing and questioning. In my experience, when a slave demonstrates resistance, Master has been inattentive; Master has not been hearing/seeing/feeling the slave's signals for help/ relief on some front. This upset can be an opportunity for Master to practice their listening skills. To derive root causes (rather than outward expressions of unhappiness): Master will need to prove he/ she understands the world through the slave's eyes.

The potential for relationship failure

The discussion about reactance and resistance edges up to a really important point. While Master/slave relationships are efficient for decision-making, they can easily become unstable. Often, it is Master's unilateral decisions that can lead to the instability. If the slave feels Master's decisions are not in the Family's best interest, there is a risk that slave may get the idea Master is discounting slave's opinions/ observations. That kind of sore will fester.

In some M/s relationships, the structure is being used as something I refer to as "The Answer System." *The Answer System* is a way of determining almost anything dealing with opinion or action. For example, it will determine…
- the truth,
- the correct thing to do,
- the right thing,
- what's real,

- what's important,
- what is a fact, and
- what should be done.

The Answer System determines all the black-and-white things about your relationship; it determines what is absolute. If you want to know what the correct answer is on any topic, just ask Master. Of course, some Masters seem to act as though they believe that it's "against the rules" to ask for the slave's view on some matter, but I'd guess they don't remain Master very long.

Master's **position** (and the *structure* of the M/s relationship) determines the point-of-view selected. It's Master's ball game. This means if the slave repeatedly observes Master making decisions in favor of Master's *wants* while disregarding slave's *needs*, the slave may begin to wonder whether this person is as competent a Master as slave hoped. The slave may begin testing Master's authority and control by subtle forms of revolt.

The relationship breakdown has begun.

All slaves revolt

All slaves revolt. It's simply historical fact. You just never know when. Since Masters realize their slave has volunteered to serve them, they are generally sensitive to signs of discontent. Master has to assess the signal slave may be sending. Is slave testing Master's boundaries? Is slave having a playful bratty streak? Is slave actually sending a distress call to Master? Perhaps slave is just trying to let Master know that the task assigned by Master exceeds slave's skill level. slave may need Master's help or additional training and doesn't feel comfortable admitting it. Possibly, slave has been put off after having tried unsuccessfully to point this out to Master. There are many possibilities; here are a few more:

- The assigned task is clearly not in the slave's best interests. This has confused or hurt the slave, as slave thought Master was responsible for acting in the slave's best interest.
- Master may have asked slave to do some task conflicting with the slave's desires to spend time with Master. So, slave does a

quick (but not thorough) job in order to be done with it. Master sees the poor job and is angry. slave just wants to be with Master and now has an upset Master who didn't understand slave's underlying love message.

- Resistance and reactance to Master may be slave's way of expressing a far deeper concern about some aspect of the relationship. Reactance can occur when you feel your safety and authority are being unfairly taken away from you.

- slave seeks more guidance and leadership than Master is providing. Mater may not have adequate leadership skills or the right personality for this particular slave.

People bring all kinds of backgrounds and experiences into their relationships. Leadership experience varies; people express authority in differing ways. For example, while vanilla partners at one end of this spectrum interact with nearly equal status, those living at the other end of the spectrum—such as those living in a Master/slave structure—maintain a strong role separation. At the Master/slave end, it would not be unusual for Master to require slave to ask permission even to go to the bathroom.

While popular fiction depicts slave serving Master's every whim, slaves need a break, too. Those in subordinate positions constantly weigh the costs and benefits for remaining in a relationship. For this reason, Master can ensure a happy household by checking occasionally with slave to confirm their needs are being met.

Other issues may concern a slave. Since our American culture so heavily promotes autonomy and freedom of personal choice, some slaves become concerned about losing themselves in their Master. They rebel in order to retain their sense of self. Whether or not you've structured your M/s dynamic to permit the slave to maintain an independent sense of self is not for me to say; I'm just providing viewpoints and perspectives. If this comes up as an issue, you may wish to revisit the purpose of your relationship and obtain a recommitment along those lines.

Rebellion, even minor rebellion, is the slave's signal of some unmet need or want. It's the early warning bell Master needs to focus on the deeper meaning of the issue-at-hand.

With all this as background, let's tackle the concept of *punishment.*

Punishment

A slave's mastery depends on *focus, intent,* and *mindset,* and their worst fear is of disappointing Master. Here's a truth for Masters: When you screw up, you own it; when your slave screws up, you own it. Virtually every failure on slave's part represents Master's *failure to train* or *failure to nurture.*

So here's the question: Why would you want to punish someone who has volunteered to serve you?

"Punishment" is a major theme in many BDSM relationships. However, there's punishment and then there's *punishment.* Here are some insights that I picked up from Master Stephen at last year's GWNN Bash in Austin.

- Punishment induces secrecy. If slave believes Master will punish certain behaviors, the threat, itself, will encourage slave to hide that specific behavior and related behaviors as well. Relationship harmony is threatened by punishment: it discourages open sharing.
- Pragmatically, the stated intention to punish is (by itself) a vote of "no-confidence" in your slave's behavior and is likely to destabilize the relationship.
- Punishment does not teach responsibility: punishment traps the punisher into monitoring the slave, looking for slave's lapses. Master is enslaved by their rules. Worse, Master now looks for negatives (rather than positives) in the slave. This condition probably signals the relationships end.
- Punishment teaches one what NOT to do, but not WHAT to do.
- *Correction* can work—the carrot-and-stick idea—so long as the carrot is something more than "not stick." You have to have positive rewards, not just absence of negative sanctions.
- Concerning the ratio of good-to-bad comments…
  - To sustain a positive relationship, you need a ratio of

about 20:1 good-to-bad comments.
- o Couples in therapy have about an 8:1 ratio of good-to-bad comments.
- o Divorcing couples have about a 1:2 ratio.

Our community is split over the topic of *punishment*. One camp says: "I am Master, you are slave: obey me or I'll beat you." The other camp says: "I am Master, you are slave: obey me and I'll beat you after dinner as a special treat." It's a basic schism over relationship dynamics.

> Managing a slave perfectly is like playing an instrument perfectly; beating a violin won't make it play better.

I distinguish between punishment and correction. It's always seemed to me one punishes an ethical breach, a breach of trust, but one *corrects* minor transgressions or protocol violations. In my view, "corrections" are a form of retraining.

I'm cautious about the entire concept of "punishment" within consensual authority-imbalanced structures. I'm leery because the s-type has volunteered to serve, and (as a general rule) works extremely hard at it. In my opinion, correction and punishment should be used very sparingly lest the slave becomes overcritical of their own actions and wary of Master's scrutiny. **I also recommend Master be particularly careful to distinguish between correcting slave's behavior versus correcting slave as a person.** You want

---

Punishment is discipline that prevents further punishment.

—SlaveMaster

---

to love and cherish the person while correcting behavior.

Punishment System
Some Masters live in anticipation: they fear that rebellion will destabilize their relationship. Such Masters tend to see *punishment* as a way to quell rebellion and improve stability. That won't work.

Punishment *comes* in two fundamental forms, but they both have the common goal of creating painful consequences if slave does not accede to Master's view about something.

Push downward: Downward punishment involves lowering the slave's rank or status. It includes shaming, ridiculing, put-downs, humiliation, derogation, and so forth. The shaming can be implied or obvious. Subtle: "Had I asked you to do that?" More obvious: "You don't have the authority within our relationship to do that!" Clear humiliation: "You're now in *time out.* You know where to go. Your nose will never be more than six inches from the black 'X' on the wall."

Downward pressure also includes lowering the person's rank within some hierarchy or structure. For example, Master may remove some areas that were previously slave's responsibility. Or, Master may restrict or remove some privilege, such as Internet access.

By the way, the *threat* of punishment is just as effective as actual punishment. The brain is designed to recall things that precede pain; it learns to react to the warning of pain as quickly as to the resulting pain. Of course, that's why *operant conditioning* works. (*Operant conditioning* is the process of changing behavior through a system of rewards and punishments.)

Push outward: "Outward punishment" occurs when you disconnect (or threaten to disconnect) slave from the relationship or the community. We have many words for this. One is fired from a company or discharged from the Military. In a marriage, it is the refusal to talk, separation, or (ultimately) divorce. Again, all these consequences can be threatened overtly or covertly with equal effect.

Resolution

Complications lurk around punishments. Yes, you must hold your slave accountable for their actions, but you're going to have to be able to "flatten" the emotional residue both from the triggering **incident** and from the correction or punishment. These are quite separate issues.

It can be a challenge to prevent memories of conflicts and corrections from leaving lasting scars. While some corrections/punishments are resolutions in their own right, there are going to be times when you'll need to do more work to discover and resolve the triggering issue(s). This is particularly true for conflicts within your relationship that just don't feel "right" or settled even after the correction/punishment is over.

Although we strive to live transparently and authentically, we all have feet of clay. When a situation has escalated to the *punishment* point, what we actually say out loud has to make it through many layers of coded meaning, projected interpretation, overly sensitive emotions, and damaged hopes. Our words may be taken in ways we didn't intend; we may not be able to say the words we wish. What comes out of our mouths may be only a portion of what we really feel. We may even express the opposite of our deeply guarded internal feelings. Emotional stress behaves that way.

Unfortunately, this condition can become a self-fulfilling prophesy. As the days/weeks/months and even years roll on, people tend to build strong barriers after core upsets: they learn to hide themselves better. Your partner, realizing (at some level) you are hiding something will reciprocate by imposing a little more emotional distance. You, picking up on the emotional distance, will redouble your own emotional protection. Your relationship is in a downward spiral. Many break-ups occur because we do not know how to get to our inner depth, or getting to it, how to share it. What we want to say isn't what comes out of our mouths.

So: how in the world does Master reach resolution with slave after an episode serious enough to require punishment? Actually, I can't answer that question. Master's conflict resolution method will depend upon their leadership style and emotional intelligence as much as on the nature of the triggering episode and slave's response to the correction/punishment. Regardless of the path taken, little is likely to change until the two (or more) of you are prepared to express and respect one another's deeper feelings, beliefs, and fears.

(Suggestion: you might want to explore ways of using "talking sticks" for serious conversations. If you're unfamiliar with talking sticks, you can look it up on the Internet. I like the *talking stick* process because it removes the emotional component from discussions. Master is more likely to obtain real answer to "off limits" questions when the exchange is done calmly. Discussions go better when the sun is shining, and the world has taken on a rosier hue than it had in the immediate aftermath of whatever happened between you. By the way, I've covered the talking stick process in my earlier book: *Master/slave Relations: Communications 401—living in harmony.*)

Atonement and absolution

You've done something you feel violated your pledge within the context of your M/s structure. You feel awful about it. You're emotionally traumatized with regret. You feel you *must* do something to make up for what you did. This line of thinking might lead you to explore the idea of *atonement.*

As Master Michael points out, *atonement* is a special-use tool. Master cannot order their slave to atone for something; the slave must request it for their own peace of mind. The concept of atonement is closely allied with the concept of making amends and then being absolved of guilt. *Atonement* has two components: first, the penitent *must* perform some act of reconciliation that satisfies the offended party; second, the penitent *must* reveal their contrition. Figuratively speaking, "contrition" means our spirit has been crushed by something regretful we've done (a misdeed, a betrayal, or even a sin or a violation of trust within the context of your M/s structure). Beyond "crushed," though, you can only get to *contrition* (and hence to *atonement*) if you feel compelled to do something about it.

Atonement discussion can be delicate and lengthy. It may take a lot of discussion to determine the root causes of your upsets. Reasons for behaviors often are well buried and hard to uncover. People do things for seemingly senseless reasons; careful, probing questions can reveal how something that started with good intentions turned out to go so wrong.

Or… did it start out with good intentions? If the intentions were not good to begin with, there is going to be a lot to talk about. Ultimately, though, the challenge is to craft an action your partner agrees will release the built-up emotions concerning the triggering episode. You have to reach agreement about the merit of your proposed atonement in order to achieve absolution. This is not always possible.

Self-recrimination and emotional upset can linger long after an event has occurred. Sometimes, the entire relationship is contaminated because the offended party was so deeply wounded by their partner's behavior. The triggering incident can be large (broken trust) or small (spilling wine at a formal dinner party). It's not the severity of the episode that matters; what matters is your partner's response. In cases where your partner is not letting go of the upset, the *atonement and absolution* path may help.

I'll end the chapter on that note.

Chapter 5: Little bits of ideas

Interacting with yourself and with others

Creating your world

Whether Master or slave, the way you talk to yourself governs your reactions to the world around you. Behavioral scientists Shad Helmstetter (author of such books as: *What to Say When you Talk to Your Self, Who Are You Really, and What Do You Want?* and, *The Self-Talk Solution*), has developed a method of readjusting your relationship with yourself.

According to Helmstetter, as much as 77% of everything we think is negative and works against your own best interests. Concurrently, says Helmstetter, medical research reveals up to 75% of all illnesses are self-induced. Overall, he concludes the brain simply believes what we most often tell it. It will create whatever we tell it about ourselves. It has no choice. It doesn't matter whether we believe it or not.

Cutting to the chase, Helmstetter shows how reprogramming your self-image will dramatically change the ways you behave and interact with others. He says, "The more you think about *yourself* in a certain way, the more you will think about yourself in that *same certain way.* The more you think about *anything* in a certain way the more you will believe that is how it really is. The brain always tries to tie new thoughts to something that you already believe."

Chapter 5: Little bits of ideas

Success or failure in managing/controlling our lives depends upon five natural steps, according to Helmstetter. Awareness of the steps improves your chances of gaining control over yourself. They are:

Behavior: How we act and what we do on a moment-by-moment basis. "Good outcomes" result from the correct series of ethically right actions.

Feelings: Actions are filtered through our feelings. How we feel about something governs our responses to it.

Attitudes: Our attitudes represent our perspectives on every topic. How we approach life (specifically, how we approach work and relationships) depends strongly on our attitudes about it, whatever the "it" is. Our beliefs create, control, or influence our attitudes according to Helmstetter.

Beliefs: Your brain does not require a belief to be true; your brain only requires you to *believe* it's true. Thus, what we have come to believe about something or somebody or even what we believe about our own capabilities has no particular relationship with objective truth: it's just what we've come to believe. Here's a question for you: Are your beliefs *assets* or *liabilities*?

Programming: Just like computers, we believe what we have been programmed since childhood to believe:
- programming creates beliefs;
- beliefs create attitudes;
- attitudes create feelings;
- feelings determine actions; and
- actions create results.

That's how the brain works. If you want to manage yourself in a better way (and change the results you've been getting) you can do so at any time you choose. Start with the first step. Choose to change your programming. Rather than describe his material in this book, I urge you to look him up: *ShadHelmstetter.com.*

I have used his techniques. I identified my own negative self-talk, carefully revised the negatives into positive statements and recording them. Then, I played them back to myself while commuting to-and-from work. Over the course of a few months, I noticed a positive difference in my outlook on life. I believe I'm a happier person as a result.

Actions always produce outcomes. Only you can choose to act to change your life.

Reacting to others

How you interact with others reveals your character: My father would often say: "We are put on this earth to help see people through, not to see through people." This relates to judging and gossiping about others. The lesson is this: When you say something unflattering to someone about another person, those hearing you know at some level you will betray them, too.

Now, so far as relating with others, here are some additional thoughts.

Expectation can set you up for disappointment. This idea came from Master Dennis (Fet = Master-Dennis) when Jen and I were speaking with him during our Butchmann's Experience in October, 2013. As I wrote down his comment, I asked him to expand upon it. Here's what he said:

> "When you expect something from someone, you limit other possible outcomes because your expectation defines what you think you want. It can be hard for you to see/consider other options and opportunities—particularly if they come from a different logic base. Your assumptions are limiting your world. To avoid that, and to get personal growth, try focusing on others."

This theme—that expectation can set you up for surprises—plays out in relationships until the Master realizes the logic loop and can to break it. Here is an example of such a loop.

Chapter 5: Little bits of ideas

- Master wants "A through Z" from their slave (or, the slave expects the M/s relationship to include "A through Z" from their Master; you can work this problem either way, of course.);
- The slave is not sure they can give A-Z but is pretty sure they can get to Q. So they agree to the A-Z package, thinking if they can get all the way to Q (or maybe even before Q), Master will be satisfied and accept what gifts they *can* offer.
- When Master does not reinforce for the letters E, G, H, etc. (because Master has forgotten they were in the initial negotiation, or now is less concerned about them), the slave becomes disillusioned and their progress falters. They become disillusioned, because Master had asked for E, G, and H but now doesn't seem to care whether the slave does those actions or not. The slave is thinking: "Where did my Master go? Has Master given up on me?"

This loop can evolve if one or both of you builds false or unclear expectations and now have to wrestle with personal compromise. Personal compromise eats away at relationships. I'd certainly suggest the two of you speak about unmet expectations. I'd also urge you to develop the practice of *gratitude.* Often, expression gratitude for what you have moves your focus away from what you're missing.

Here's another word of M/s caution: Only expect from your partner what they are capable of giving to the relationship. People have emotional, physical, mental, and imaginary limits. Yes, you can help them overcome their self-imposed limits, but in this regard the first rule is: Don't set them up to failure. Make a habit of "catching" your partner doing something really well or special. You, yourself, will reap the rewards of building up your partner's self-confidence and self-esteem.

Sometimes you have to let people go. Not all relationship issues can be resolved. Sometimes, you have to let people go so they will be able to develop differently than they can by living with you. Sometimes, you have to let people go because they are damaging you, yourself. Relationships change; people change. The relationship that was successful ten years ago may not function as well now. We all know the "letting go" process is very scary and emotionally traumatic. However, sometimes it is the right thing to do as the compassionate and loving partner. I'm particularly sensitive to this point, as I'm 20 years older than Jen: at some point, it's in her best interest if she finds someone younger to serve her. That's simply the reality. In my world, it's part of living in integrity: I've pledged to serve and to obey. At some point, I'll no longer be able to serve.

> Only the mind can create errors. Truths are not created, they exist; one can see them, disentangle them, discover them, and expose them.
>
> —Joseph Joubert

Reframing

Reframing **enables you to see possibilities:** Couples get stuck. One person forms an opinion (or conclusion) about the other person without discussing the issue with them. It's natural. However, there is a process taught to those studying Neuro-Lingusitic Programming (NLP) to help break through stuckness. It's called *reframing*. Reframing is a large and deep topic; you may wish to find out more about it if these few examples spark your interest. Jen and I teach quite a bit of NLP material in our conference and club presentations. There are many, many times when Master or slave hears the other person say something jarring and need a way to re-think it. NLP offers the tools to do just that. I'll touch on a few of them in this section, but I strongly urge you to reach out and learn more about NLP: all aspects of your life will benefit. That's a promise.

Now: to "reframe" something is to turn it around from negative wording (or thinking) to positive wording (or thinking). This is a crucial first step to changing your world outlook from negative to positive. Reframes come in two categories: *content* reframes and *context* reframes. Here are a few examples:

From: Why is this happening to me?
To: What can I learn from this?
Or: What's really funny about this I haven't seen?

From: Master is micromanaging me!
To: Master cares about me so much they are taking extra time to point out ways to do this task.
Or: I really am looking forward to meeting my new self once I learn all Master is teaching me.

From: All Master's ongoing critiques make me crazy; I just can't seem to please Master.
To: Wow! Now I understand why this M/s Path is so demanding and why so few choose it. What an honor to be afforded this opportunity.

You get to take it from here. Write down the negatives and fears ("hot buttons") that are bothering/upsetting you, then work together to derive the reframes. You're likely to find the very act of identifying your upsets helps the two of you to talk about them.

Strategies for helping someone change their beliefs: M/s relationship structures aren't culturally supported. We lack good reference models. As a result, each couple brings unique opinions and beliefs into our M/s world. These opinions and beliefs have developed from our own upbringing and life experiences. Sometimes, our beliefs hinder us in our relationship. Sometimes, we may need to help our partner examine their established beliefs to verify they are, in fact, beliefs—in contrast to cultural assumptions. NLP can help with this.

I'm going to start this section assuming you already know something about how to establish and maintain *rapport* with someone. If not, you might wish to do some research into NLP techniques and acquire those skills.

Once in rapport, then:
- Assume the person can do what they say they can do at some level of proficiency.

- Ask questions aimed at uncovering the positive intention or purpose of the belief you're trying to understand. Why does this person believe this? What good does this belief serve them?
- Acknowledge whatever is going on for the person; don't pretend their reality doesn't exist.
- Determine the structure of the belief: when do they use this belief? How "solid" is it? Are there exceptions to when this belief can be used?
- Understand that beliefs are formed very early in life and are closely tied to self-protection and physical/emotional survival. It can be very difficult to piece together the basis of someone's beliefs. It is important to maintain rapport during your conversation, because discussions to explore the meanings of closely-held beliefs can become very emotional. You may have to withdraw from your line of questions and re-focus on your connection and rapport if the conversation becomes too intense.
- Recognize that beliefs are perceptions. What someone believes to be "real" or "the truth" is so for them. The mind can't determine whether something is objectively real or subjectively real. Both appear to be true to them.

Again, this isn't the place to teach you the subtleties of NLP. I'm just trying to get you to consider reading a bit about, as I consider it a valuable resource for those of us in M/s structures.

Strategies for reframing disappointment: Let's imagine the unimaginable; you specifically told slave to do X and they didn't do it. It's a big deal—it has affected your trust in your slave. You have some options, depending on your personality, your slave's personality, and the specific situation. I'll just touch on a few.

First, you can take the overall position your slave would never willfully disobey you. You can use this as a personal learning experience. If so, you can reframe the episode and ask yourself: "What do I yet have to learn about the way I give orders and the way my slave hears my orders to avoid a recurrence of this mess?" From such a perspective, you can now ask a lot of questions. For example, you might wish to examine how you phrase requests, orders, and instructions. Alternatively, you might wish to explore techniques to help your slave do a better job monitoring itself, particularly in areas where their decisions could affect the relationship.

Second, you can take the overall position that trust is something *given* in contrast to something *earned.* This is slightly different from passively waiting for someone to earn your trust; this viewpoint means you are actively responsible for deciding how much trust to give someone.

Psychologically, this approach is a kissing-cousin to the generally-accepted view that *you can't change someone else, you can only change your reaction to the person.* When someone does something differently than you expected (usually something negative), you have the opportunity to choose to recommit to your own journey. Remember the aphorism: "Everything that happens is an opportunity to go to the next opportunity."

If you're still with me, here's the kicker: "It" already makes sense; the only challenge is to figure out how "it" fits in with "what is" for you. If you see "it" as "wrong," you miss the fact that "it" is a blessing. (Closing my "Woo Book" now, and reopening the psych book.)

Hedonic adaptation comes into play when discussing ways of reframing disappointments. In brief, this evolving theory proposes that people have a unique set-point on their happiness/unhappiness scale. This set-point is independent of external circumstances (such as winning the lottery or having your house burn down). People bounce back to their "good-old-selves" pretty quickly after being surprised with unusually good or bad news, according to set-point theory. I'd argue that the same is generally true when it comes to Master or slave disappointing one another. Since you each probably know you're going to survive this localized upset, you might as well prepare for disappointments.

Rethinking meanings

Some M/s workshop presenters try to tackle the more controversial and tricky concepts such as the meaning of "no," the subtleties of value words, or ways of identifying the shadow side of one's personality. I'm going to leave "no" and Jungian psychology out of this section and spend just a little time examining some words we believe we know so well that turn out to be pretty interesting when applied to M/s.

Honor: Master's honor keeps slave safe. They are linked, because *honor* is closely linked to *trust* and *integrity*. As a slave, you want to hear your Master saying such things as: "I wouldn't ever do that because it's contrary to who I am and to my code of conduct."

I'd go out on a limb, here and propose in an M/s relationship **love** isn't the core issue; the core issue is **honor**. The *love* discussion gets confused with *Eros*: being "in love." Master must hold firm to their love for their slave in order to be able to guide the slave through situations they find difficult, even though you believe the assigned task/ordeal is in their best interest.

Risk: There is always risk: there is even risk in doing nothing. If you find a Path seemingly risk-free, chances are it's so safe you can't learn much you don't already know about yourself and your fellow man. It's about the same with obstacles blocking paths: if a path has no obstacles, chances are it doesn't lead anywhere interesting.

> I do not believe in a fate that falls on men *however they act*; but I do believe in a fate that falls on them *unless* they act.
>
> —G.K. Chesterton

Now, most of us are seeking our own description of "a good life." This description usually includes such words as: calm, stable, filled with love and acceptance, a reasonable job, comfortable housing, and adequate transportation. Interestingly, it's the *good* things in life that keep us from seeking the great things. This happens either because we grow complacent and stop looking, or because we fear losing (or

Chapter 5: Little bits of ideas

destabilizing) the "good" we already have. In either case, most of us are generally closed to experiences that stretch our comfort levels.

It's a little like the reality that we stop looking for something once we find it. After all, why keep looking: you already found it. While that works for "things," it is less effective when it comes to experiences and people. You see a small version of this dichotomy with people on FetLife. Some people put restrictions on who may "friend" them (they must have met, or they must have a reference) while others accept all friend requests on the principle that one can never be too rich, too healthy, or have too many friends.

This applies to M/s. The relationship grows and matures as Master pushes themselves and their slaves to learn and experience new things.

Trust: Trust = honesty + integrity + respect. Trust and respect are at the heart of M/s relations. As Sergeant Major pointed out to me in 2011 at South Plains Leatherfest, *conferring trust* is an active process, "Trust entails an act. We execute an 'act of trust,' something is given by one party and received by another." He goes on to say: "When conferred, *trust* undergoes a metamorphosis. What begins as trust when it leaves the donor becomes converted to power when accepted by the recipient. Actively trusting an individual or group is giving them a degree of power over oneself."

Sergeant Major provides a caveat: "Trust can be earned or obtained by deception. The difference lies in whether the recipient uses it to reciprocate and benefit, or exploits it for personal gain. As words such as *honor, trust,* and *loyalty* and even *courtesy* can mean different things to different people, I strongly urge you to go through the exercise of writing out what these mean in the context of your own M/s relationship. Again quoting from Sergeant Major: "Chivalry (in the form of courtesy) and courtliness can have a potent appeal to the modern mind. It offers ritual, color, pageantry and spectacle to a world largely devoid of those things. Having an established hierarchy of values and a code of conduct, trust can be made to come alive to communicate your meaning to others both through your words and resulting actions. It can demonstrate your thoughtfulness to others who are part of your community."

Self-delusion

> Your agreement with reality defines your life.
>
> —Steve Maraboli

Delusion is everywhere. Your reality depends heavily on your lifetime of experiences as well as your attitude towards life in general. In this section, I want to bring up a contemporary concept from the world of psychology. It's the concept of *cognitive dissonance resolution* initially developed in the late 1950s by Stanford Professor Carl Festinger. Festinger noticed when someone's actions are inconsistent with their own beliefs, they realize it, feel a discord (dissonance) and try to resolve it. Minor conflicts may simply be dismissed as insignificant (e.g., putting a pen in your pocket as you're leaving the bank teller's window and not realizing it until you're in your car). However, violating one of your own life-principles will make you noticeably upset with yourself. Your personal reaction depends upon how important the principal was that you violated, and how seriously you violated it. In any case, according to the theory, the more your lapse has upset you, the more you will be motivated to resolve it.

Discord of this sort is resolved in one of three ways:
- the person can change their beliefs to be congruent with their actions;
- the person can change their actions to be congruent with their beliefs:
- the person can rationalize their actions.

We get in trouble with this last area, the area of self-justification. As you reflect on the upsetting episode, you start to think about it in a different manner or context. Slowly, your memory of the event starts to shift. Eventually, what you did no longer appears to be inconsistent with your

beliefs. Here are some examples:
- The test you cheated on was for a dumb class that you didn't really need. Anyway, everyone cheats so why not you?
- You cheat on your partner because they don't give you the kind of sex (or as much sex) you want. Besides, who'll know? It's not **your** fault your partner doesn't want sex with you anymore.
- You're lucky they fired you: you hated working around those assholes. And the management sucked. They did you a favor!

Here's the self-justification pattern phrased in more everyday terms:
- Something happens between two people.
- Each person creates a story that supports their own needs.
- These stories are different.
- People listening to the two versions will believe the person they like the best, or who retells their version of the story most vocally.

If you reflect on this series of mental gymnastics for a moment you will probably recognize why cognitive dissonance has come to be so popular. If you're like me, you notice other people engaging in such *post-hoc* reconceptualizations (rationalizations), though it's not as common to see it in one's self.

Cognitive dissonance resolution helps to explain a great deal about the stories you hear bandied about in our community. Someone gets hurt or angry, becomes embarrassed about how they acted, but are too proud (or self-centered) to apologize. This is where you come in: this is where you can continue to offer empathy and understanding. Shower your enemies with love. It confuses them. They may have to go back and reevaluate the story they made up about you.

The more general truth is this: your mind will do about anything to avoid taking responsibility for its actions.

Service

If serving is below you, leadership is beyond you.

Over the past few years, a saying has grown up in the M/s community that I've previously mentioned. The saying is: slave serves Master; Master serves the relationship. Now, I can't tell you what "serving Master" or "serving the relationship" means. These are concepts unique to each relationship and derive their meaning from the relationship's **purpose.** The best I can do in this book is to point out that Master has an obligation to keep the purpose of the relationship in mind when giving instructions and when giving corrections or punishments to their slave.

"Purpose?" you ask. Sure: some people will form M/s relationships as a means of developing a deep and spiritual relationship; others will become involved in M/s in order simply to serve or be served (without much need for emotional nurturing). There are diverse and interesting reasons people give for entering into M/s structures. This is important to think about, for your particular reason for being a Master or a slave affects your expectations. Expectations govern reactions. You react to your partner's words and deeds through your filter of expectations. Master might seek certain kinds of service from their slave; slave may expect their Master to feed the relationship with emotional energy. Until you work these out, your interactions may be a little rocky.

Intention precedes service

Discussions about *intentions* go hand-in-hand with topics such as mindfulness and presence. Actually, I would argue that *successful service* is a blend of *intent, mindfulness,* and *presence.*

The intention behind an act of service (the *why of* it) is often more important than the service, itself (the *what* of it). "Providing service" is different from "providing requested service." It's actually worse than that: actions performed automatically or without much thought simply because you mean well, or because it's how *you* would wish to be served may not feel right to Master. In fact, service not considering the other person's needs is merely wasted effort, so far as your relationship is concerned.

I'll give you a real-time personal example. The other day at work (as I went to make myself a cup of coffee) I noticed my CEO had left her newly brewed coffee in the coffee machine. I took it to her and asked

Chapter 5: Little bits of ideas

whether she would like me to warm it in the microwave oven. Wow! Did I get an earful: "We're at work; you're not at home serving Jen. Thank you for bringing my coffee, but it's not your role in this company to warm my coffee. If I want it warmed, I'll do it myself."

What just happened? What happened was I failed to get out of my own "making coffee for the person I serve loop" and consider the history of needs of the person I was actually serving. I failed to review what I knew about my CEO. For example, I knew:

- my CEO wants Alpha-types around her, not service types;
- she doesn't like other people doing things for her; and
- I actually knew (had I stopped to think about it) she doesn't like hot beverages or food.

I should have realized she would not react well to an offer to warm her coffee, but I didn't. I remained in my own comfort zone, acted mindlessly, and got my hand slapped.

Back to M/s: if slave is doing something mindlessly, I would argue they have changed their role from "slave" to "servant." As I previously mentioned, servants fulfill their employers' *needs* while slaves fulfill their Master's *wants*. To remain a slave to a Master means to focus your intentions on the honor of your service. For Master to continue to be served by this slave, they must make their needs clear (to avoid the slave acting out of its own willfulness, even in an effort to please). Always remember Raven Kaldera's theme: *If Master doesn't want it, it's not service.*

For slaves, this raises such issues as how they make the bed and how they do the dishes as much as it has to do with how they put on makeup or what clothing they select to wear.

As the slave's specific intentions within their own relationship are unknown to an outsider, I can only offer some high-level observations.

- Change happens in your life when you stop craving control over areas Master has restricted and take control of areas where you actually *do* have power.

- Choice is made visible through action. Action is animated by your intentions. Translation: being demonstrably happy as you carefully wash each plate, cup, glass, and tableware because your focus is on the honor of washing the dishes from which your Master has dined is a world apart from throwing dishes into a dish-washer while cleaning the kitchen in "cleaning-the-kitchen" autopilot mode. The results are similar, but the first approach keeps slave in slave head space and reinforces the M/s bond.
- Happiness is not the absence of problems; *death* is the absence of problems. Happiness is being alive and having the ability to deal with problems. Focus on the gratitude for another day of life with your Master or slave and the time that has been given you to deal with your challenges.

Intention needs *attention*

As my father used to say: "You have to keep your eye on the ball." In M/s speak, this would be: "You have to keep your eye on the purpose (intent) of your relationship."

"Trouble" can build in relationships as the years roll on. The form or structure won't matter: you can get to know someone too well. Focusing on M/s relationships, I suspect dissatisfaction builds as faded hopes collide with missed opportunities. The process of learning how to live together in this unusual type of relationship can wear people out. Many important lessons come at the cost of collateral emotional damage that affects the couple's future. People change as they gain M/s experience. Among other things, as their understanding of M/s changes, their understanding about respective roles can change. These metamorphoses sometimes give rise to dreams of having a Master/slave with different skills or with a different personality. For some couples, the Master's idea about owning a slave no longer meshes with owning this specific slave. Likewise, I'm sure there are slaves for whom the fantasy/image of being owned and cherished doesn't mesh well with being owned and cherished by this particular Master.
Of course, some M/s couples have better communication skills than others, and many are used to working through discord as it arises. For them, most issues are resolved or accommodated, and life is good.

Chapter 5: Little bits of ideas

However, at the other end of the spectrum, joy has gone and the slave is completing assigned tasks with a heavy heart. Unfortunately for this couple, mutually-gratifying sexual pleasure is a thing of the past.

There is a saying in the world of M/s dynamics: I've slipped into this book a few times. *Master's wants cannot trump slave's needs.* Most experienced Masters (*e.g.,* who have lived with the same slave for over five years) have learned their need to serve the larger relationship. They have learned how to provide slave both physical and emotional safety so slave can relax into service knowing they are protected. Part of that protection involves Master's responsibility for ensuring as many misunderstandings as possible are made visible and discussed openly; it is Master's responsibility to pull the emotional loading out of areas that have become relationship hotspots.

By way of a suggestion, Masters reading this book might consider sitting down and writing out their needs in quantifiable terms. For example, you know you need to feel loved, honored, and respected, but how does that translate so your slave knows how to make you feel loved, honored, and respected? What do the words mean to you? How strongly do you feel about each one? How are these terms expressed in ways that you'll recognize them? You might consider creating a written list of issues/areas where you have personal needs, and work with your slave to develop protocols of the ways slave's service fuels those needs. For Masters who have themselves served as a slave, ask yourself: what challenges did you find that you'd now like your slave to avoid?

Much of the prior paragraph applies equally to slaves. What form of service sings to your heart? How do you quantify that service? Have you discussed (or updated) your own long-term needs with your Owner? Do they support your needs in the context of your service? Are there certain areas of living in the subordinate position that concern/alarm you? If you had some fairy dust to sprinkle over your Master that would absolutely change their behavior in any way you specifically instructed, what specific instructions would you give your Master?
Food for thought, yes?

Service as a concept

In the context of a modern Master/slave relationship, *service* can involve some tricks and twists. You have to work through these tricks and twists before you can get to the treats of service. In my experience, *receiving service* requires some forethought. I had to work through some fundamental issues in my own relationships in order to determine how I wanted to be served (by my then-slave) and how I needed to serve (my current Owner).

The kind of service you want depends upon how you define your relationship's *purpose*. For example, some Master's use their slave to fulfill their personal wants; other Masters use their slave to augment their own skills and influence. One is not better than the other, but the kind of service is likely to be different for those two approaches.

The first step, then, is to determine how you want *service* to interact with the *purpose and intent* of your relationship.

Certainly, one's version of "serving Master" or "being served by slave" depends upon a mix of variables. The way you were brought up, your life experiences, your idea of "comfortable living," and endless other topics unique to who you are individually and as a couple. You will have to choose the specific role(s) you expect your slave to fulfill as you refine your personalized version of *service*. Here are some ideas to start you thinking:

- I really want a polite, devoted partner who does what I ask of them.
- I want a "personal assistant" to help me in my work (whether such work is on a farm or in an office).
- I want a *major domo* who runs the household (and manages the other slaves).
- I want a "courtesan" who is graceful, socially savvy, artistic, and musical to occupy my nights.
- I want someone who will support our Family's dedication to serve our Leather/kink community.

Once you can name *why* the two (or more) of you are together, then you can start to refine ways *service* can be made real for everyone involved.

Forms of service

How do you want to be served? Do you even care? I would argue that without specific directions, a slave is likely to act on their own to fill the void of leadership. The "void of leadership" can arise for many reasons. slaves may feel Master simply isn't being adequately specific about what they want the slave to do. Master may not have thought through how they really want to be served. They *could* ask slave to do X, Y, or Z, but it never dawned on them. Master has no model to draw upon. Unless they have grown up in a tight-knit "old-school" gay leather community, or have been exposed to the Mistress/ProDomme community, or have been a part of the M/s community through MAsT, they seldom see other Masters, and their imaginations are limited because of cultural conditioning.

Translation: your neighbors aren't modeling M/s; your parents aren't modeling M/s; the public media isn't supporting M/s. When it comes to developing service protocols as a vehicle to strengthen your M/s bond, you're on your own. It works better for some than for others. If you share my view about using service protocols to strengthen your relationship, here are some resources to consider:

- *Service Etiquette, 5th Edition,* by Cherlynn Conetsco and Anna Hart (This book is the definitive resource of military protocol. Our State Department and major corporations who deal with the international community use this book. Not only is it fun to read, but it's a core book for those following the military model of M/s);

- *The Butler Speaks: A guide to stylish entertaining, etiquette, and the art of good housekeeping* by Charles MacPherson and *The Butler's Guide to Running the Home and Other Graces* by Stanley Ager and Fiona St. Aubyn (In a clear, straightforward style, Charles MacPherson lays out the essentials of entertaining and household management in this beautifully illustrated style, etiquette and entertainment guide. The book includes everything you need to know to simplify, organize and care for your home. It also offers modern advice on personal style and etiquette. It's essential reading if you wish your slave to be your butler).

If Master wishes the Family to learn and use table manners a notch above casual dining, a simple "table manners" search on Amazon or Barnes and Noble produces many options. If Master wishes the household to learn *formal* dining manners, then I'd recommend *A Butler's Guide to Table Manners* by Nicholas Clayton. (This book covers all aspects of eating etiquette, from napkin folding, cutlery, glasses, bread rolls, and silver service to how to eat soup, spaghetti, artichoke, and how to open a bottle of champagne. He includes diagrams for tricky table placements and eating actions.)

Recognizing service

How will you know you are being served? This question applies equally (but differently) to Master and to slave. From Master's point of view, there may be a disconnect between *what slave is doing* and whether or not Master even cares it is being done. If Master does not care about some of their slave's actions, Master won't consider them "service." If Master continues to think the slave's actions are not the kind of service they had in mind, the relationship, itself, may be at risk.

From slave's point of view, slave may be working very hard to deliver the kind of service they (the slave) would appreciate if *they* (the slave) were being served. This leads us directly to the main point of this subsection: not everything the slave does is service. Some of slave's acts are really done by the slave for the slave. Similarly, some of what the slave does may be the slave's **projections** of what the slave thinks the Master would like or appreciate as service. Just because the *slave* thinks they are providing service doesn't make it so. To repeat a quote from about ten pages ago from Joshua Tenpenny and Raven Kaldera in their book *Real Service, "If Master doesn't want it, it's not service."* Worse, unrequested service is willful on the slave's part.

The key question for slaves: *whose needs are you serving*? Just because slave loves and wishes to serve Master does not mean their love for Master or their proffered service feeds Master's needs. Unrequested (and unwanted) "service" by slave is the M/s version of "topping from the bottom." The slave is taking control of the M/s dynamic to serve outside the scope of Master's leadership and guidance. Not a good thing for a stable long-term M/s relationship.

Masters can avoid such situations by clearly defining the "service" they expect from their slave.

Note: If you wonder about the path down which slave-instigated service can lead, I'd refer you to the "Jeeves and Wooster" television series made from British satirical novelist P.G. Wodehouse. In the novels/movies, the ever-so-clever Jeeves (Wooster's Gentleman's Gentleman) clearly runs circles around his Master under the pretext of offering *helpful suggestions.* (Granted, Wooster would make a hash of things without Jeeves, but Wooster is clearly not in command beyond being Jeeves' employer. By the way, even the title of the series/novel lists Jeeves first, reflecting the manservant's superior position within the relationship.)

Actually, this is a good place to stick in a word about *anticipatory service.* There is some controversy about anticipatory service. While some see it as the most desirable of slave traits, others are concerned that it returns too much autonomy and will to slave. This group is concerned about Master's dependence upon the slave who is serving before being asked to serve. They point out that such service creates dependency upon the server and raises the question about who is leading in the relationship. I think this is a bit extreme, but I'm reporting it because I've heard it come up a number of times.

All of this is to say: it can be useful to define *service* within your relationship in order that slave knows how to focus its actions to please Master.

Specialized communication challenges

Way back in time… in the late 1960s, in fact, Eldridge Cleaver became famous for observing: "If you are not a part of the solution, you are a part of the problem." That was a harsh thing to say in those days; it was a radical statement made by a radical thinker. Actually, Eldridge Cleaver's statement can usefully be applied to our M/s dynamic, for we live in a world where if you're not working *on* the relationship, you're really not *in* the relationship. If you are not part of the solution, you're part of the problem.

This brings us face-to-face with such topics as *attentiveness, mindfulness,* and *intent*.

We can all agree it's the slave's job to be very attentive to whatever Master is saying: no arguments, right? But… what happens if Master is not very attentive to what they are actually saying? You've been together for years and you're used to one another's speaking patterns. slave has learned to translate certain phrases; slave has learned the pattern of Master's wants. Over the last few years, speaking together has felt like speaking to a roommate; in many situations, the slave has learned to tune out Master.

I would argue that casual speech—speech not, itself, reinforcing the dynamic of authority-imbalance—works against the relationship's integrity. As Master is leading this parade, Masters' level of speech signals the formality of the relationship. In the same way that casual dress signals casual behavior, casual speech is used with equals. Personally, I would argue that casual speech is both imprecise and power-neutral. Casual speech will not help reinforce Master's leadership or the authority imbalance at the core of your relationship. I do not believe casual speech is your friend.

This entire line of irritating argument (for you're likely to argue with me over it) brings us face-to-face with *another* uncomfortable question: Do you (either as Leader/follower, Master/slave) speak to communicate a message intended to be understood and acted upon, or do you simply speak and hope for the best?
- Do our requests carry time deadlines?
- Does failure at any level trigger consequences?
- Do you realize you're drifting away from structure and towards something else?

Now, let's turn the question on its head: when you listen, do you listen to *understand*, do you listen to *respond/react*, or are you just *socializing*?

Chapter 5: Little bits of ideas

If you think your *connection* would benefit from clearer communication, you might wish to consider creating protocols to signal when you are speaking as *partners* in contrast to speaking with your *Master* or *slave.* In the alternative, you might consider living 24/7 in high protocol. It's an option.

This section examines some of the specialized challenges in communication within an M/s structure.

Basic versus stressed communication

I have already written a book about communication strategies for those who live in a Master/slave structure (*Master/slave Relations: Communications 401—the advanced course*). If you have not yet read it, you may wish to consider picking up a copy. It contains many "out-of-the-box" strategies and *work-arounds*—and it's a fun read.

However, I don't want to bring that material into *this* book, so I'll just open this section with a comment that unlike calm, quiet mutually-satisfying conversations, conversations that have become laced with stress and emotion are an entirely different beast. Depending on the particular personalities of the M/s couple, you might find it helpful to establish some communication protocols to call upon during "serious" conversations.

People tend to avoid serious conversations because they involve risks. For example, the person with the issue may be seeking a heart-felt conversation only to find the other person has become reactive either to the way their partner is approaching the topic, or to the topic being brought up at all. The reactive person may respond (to your surprise) out of fear, guilt, or shame. Also, they may only offer partial replies out of their own fear of *your* reactions. This is the "walking on eggshells" issue commonly found in dysfunctional relationships—particularly in relationships involving co-dependence. This situation can cause collateral damage. At least one of the partners now realizes they don't have a clear and safe communication channel with their partner.

Communication and expectations

When Master steps up to the plate and accepts slave as property, Master is understood now to be 100% responsible for their basic health (physical and psychological). That's an easy concept; I'd like to explore it a bit further.

Let's set the medical side apart but think about the process of becoming the owner of something. To make it practical, let's talk about buying a car. When you are about to buy a car, I suspect you would have learned quite a bit about the makes and models that interest you. I also suspect you will have read reviews of that particular make and model. You probably shopped around a little and selected accessories and options along with the engine size. When actually in the car lot, you would take it for a test drive in order to assess the engine's power and the way it handles. You would realize this is a complex and expensive piece of equipment, so perhaps you take it to your mechanic to get it checked out. All good. Now let's transfer this line of thought to selecting a partner, either M-type or s-type.

When it comes to people, there is no social model that includes taking an intended partner to a psychotherapist for a general check-up. That's probably not a problem: chances are your partner either operates within acceptable bounds, or they've described to you whatever "abnormal" condition they may have. But, have you, yourself, ever taken some of the commonly available tests such as a Myers/Briggs or a Kobe A exam to help you to understand how **you** work: Have you considered asking a potential partner take those tests to discover not only how **they** think but also how the two of you are likely to work together?

This leads us to the larger question: to what extent has Master sought to understand the complex psychological makeup of their slave in order to understand how to correctly (safely) "operate" or manage this particular piece of equipment? After all, knowing how to drive a car has little bearing on being able to drive a racecar on a high-speed track. Your slave is a racecar. At this level, structured authority-imbalanced relationships are for experienced people.

Chapter 5: Little bits of ideas

Master will want to know how slave takes in and processes information (processing modalities tests and such). Master will want to know whether slave's basic ethical values correspond to Master's values (values clarification process). Master will want to know how slave's working styles compliment Master's working style (Kobe-A test on the Internet), etc. So: if slave doesn't do something the way Master wanted it done, perhaps it's because...

- The task was not explained clearly. ("Please pick up some steak for dinner" does not reveal any facts about the kind of steak, the grade of meat, the quantity of meat, or how much per pound you should expect to spend. Disappointment, astonishment, and surprise may await your return from the store: this is *communication failure*.)
- Master didn't explain the task in a manner slave could understand. (I have Asperger Syndrome—my brain wiring isn't "neuro-typical." You may say X and I understand it as Xa and do Xa and anger you for having added in the unrequested "a." However, I did what I understood you to have asked.)
- The task involved skills/issues/areas you poorly understand (or are invisible to you because they are not part of your knowledge-set). Easy examples come from the world of gender-related upbringing: you would expect a woman to have more trouble trying to figure out how to change a car tire than a man; you'd expect a man to get lost in a beauty supply store trying to pick up some item that would be a "Duhh!" for any woman.
- You became reactive to something Master said. (Master hit a hidden landmine; you didn't even know about it and now you're reacting to it. You're upset and Master is likely to be confused by seemingly bizarre reactions to what they thought was a non-issue).
- You ethically object to Master's request.
- You have knowledge Master doesn't have so you did not or could not fulfill the order as it was put to you. Two paths immediately occur to me. First, slave failed to inform Master of the additional information and now can't say anything without revealing this; or second, Master has asked slave to do something that has emotional loading associated with it.

So, for starters, the two of you may wish some "learning-one-another" training time to be sure you're still a good fit after all these years.

Here's a strategy: you can use this phrasing when determining where the communication went wrong and you're trying to get realigned: " When I say "X" I mean "Y"; now, when I say "X", what do **you** think I mean?"

This process can help to clear up different meanings between terms or concepts. For example, consider discussing the distinction between *abandonment* and *rejection*. These words often come up when asking conference class participants for words describing a slave's greatest fears.

Conventional wisdom says *abandonment* emotions result from someone cutting you out of their lives. Someone (parent or spouse) leaves you. Your prior close emotional bonds are broken. You feel abandoned. It wasn't your fault; you may never know the cause of the abandonment. You were collateral damage. It wasn't personal.

Rejection is a different beast. *Rejection* emotions (and the resulting hit to your self esteem) are generated when one person has had a chance to evaluate you (or something you are suggesting) and concludes you (or your suggestion) doesn't meet their wants/needs. *Rejection* can take many forms. At a simple level, slave may feel rejected when Master chooses to watch TV rather than interact with them. At the serious level, Master may move their emotional bond away from you and to another person or thing.

How one does something is how one does everything

When you think about it, this is a little-known truism makes a lot of sense. As people grow up, they have (much in the sense of Darwinian Adaptation), created their own way of understanding and interacting with the world around them. They develop quite specific ways of approaching and solving issues or challenges. In the same way knowledge is based on experiences, personalities represent a compilation of coping strategies that made sense to their subconscious and were therefore integrated into their being. As a result, the way one does something is pretty much the way they do everything. It's eerie. Others will be more able to see this trait in you than you will, yourself. Too close to the forest, and all that. Master will see it in their slave; their slave will see it in their Master.

By the way, this doesn't mean the way you do things is either a good or even a successful schema. There is no value judgment; it's just the way you work. The "rub" (only slightly mangling a famous quote by Albert Einstein) is this: not every problem can be solved using the same logic set. Some problems object quite forcefully if you try to solve them with your established logic set. This is why personal flexibility becomes so important in life.

Communication assumptions

There are some large-scale assumptions that underlie discussions about *communication.* Here are three "quickies:"

- Your mind doesn't distinguish between what *really* happened and the way you've reconstructed the event as having happened. Thus, unless you are a skilled observer, your version of reality is pretty much just your own version of reality.
- Projection causes you to contaminate your interpretation of events because you project what **you** would mean if you said/ did "X" onto the person saying/doing "X."
- You make what is referred to as *the usual error.* "The usual error" is that other people think (or problem-solve) as you do.

Keeping those three assumptions in mind, here's the most general overview I know of about the consequences of communication:

Something happens >> realities get set by both parties >> meanings get assigned.

People can react to events in unusual ways. If you do "X" and get an unexpected response there's a good chance they are reacting to unknown and unresolved personal issues having little or nothing to do with you. In fact, it's quite possible this person's emotional baggage has just taken over your conversation. While I don't mean to sound melodramatic, you might wish to think about this person as *not quite in their right mind.* Their thinking may be a little irrational. In extreme cases, you may find you're saying A, B, and C while they are responding to stone, K, and hay. It's at this point that you, being on the receiving end, must be very, very careful not to further trigger this situation.

Here's the kind of conversation you want to avoid. You're in the heat of a really bad emotional meltdown. One person says: "Fine, we're done!" The listener takes this to mean the relationship is over and says: "Fine!" They gather a few belongings and leave. The first person is in astonished shock. They didn't want their partner to go; they only meant the conversation was over. The person leaving didn't really want to go, but they thought they were told to get out. There you are; both people are fuming and hurt. A mess.

Heated communications can lead to odd outcomes neither person wants. It's not that one or the other person was at fault, exactly. When two people blend their energies, they create a new entity called "the relationship." It has its own distinct energy pattern with unique challenges and opportunities. It also has its own set of communication rules. It can take a long time to figure out what they are.

On conflict

Conflicts can arise in a relationship when one person feels their self-esteem being threatened; they begin to feel less-than or belittled. This can be particularly delicate in an M/s structure where the very *purpose* of the relationship is to reinforce the power imbalance between Master and slave. So, if the s-type feels Master is abusing their authority, slave's "self-esteem controller" may call out to its buddies, *self-defense* and *anger.* Now the battle is on, and both parties realize they're in an *upset.* Leaders immediately begin to work out what they can do to restore emotional stability; those less skilled are sucked into the upset.

Wouldn't it be great if we could turn to our partner and say something like: "Sweetheart, please avert your eyes as Daddy fucks up…"

Chapter 5: Little bits of ideas

Wouldn't it be great if we could put a sign on our foreheads that reads: "Caution, Mistakes Ahead."

Yah, right.

Interestingly, examples such as those are often the easiest to manage because they are clear and obvious: you know there is an upset. More generally, it's hard even to realize you're in an emotional spiral. You are only aware you're not having fun and that you don't look forward to starting a new day. Anxiety tends to travel with friends: money problems, work problems, social problems, and relationship problems often go out drinking together. It can take professional help to sort it all out. Then, once sorted, the challenge is to figure out how to stop the spiral, gain control, and work to stabilize your life. I didn't say anything about it being easy to regain personal control; I only said that conflict often has multiple causes.

Emotional conflicts carry risks. These risks are quite different from one another. One risk occurs when one person misreads/misunderstands the root cause of the conflict. This happens, for example, if one of the people generally approaches conflicts as a "fixer" who wants "resolution" but the other person approaches conflicts as an opportunity to find a better way of working together. One person is starting out seeing a "problem" and the other person is starting out seeing an opportunity to resolve an issue (not even seen as a "problem"). These two people aren't even in the same book, let alone on the same page. The *fixer* gets more and more upset when not able to "fix" the problem but the other person is getting more and more upset at not being "heard."

The second risk has to do with the way people respond to conflict. Some people want to stay engaged until all the issues are settled; other people want to withdraw as soon as possible in order to think through what is happening. In these cases, the person who wants to remain and work through the upset may feel abandoned, unheard, or disrespected when the other person withdraws emotionally and/or physically. This compounds the situation, of course. (Note: In support of those who prefer to walk away, remember it takes 20-40 minutes for an anger or adrenaline reaction to flush through your system. Postponing the discussion should lower the risk of an emotional meltdown.)

In cases of certain kinds of conflict, the very inability to manage the conversation starts leading to a breakup. This can happen as slave watches Master lose self-Mastery. It's a sobering experience to watch your Master lose control of themselves, but emotional upsets have a way of thrusting one fully into "judgment mode" about how the other person is acting/reacting.

To avoid that path—the path where an argument becomes relationship-threatening—it helps to have pre-planned some methods to disengage before someone says something they'll regret. Master Andy and slave sue (MAsT Ottawa) have built this relevant protocol: "We won't make a decision about the structure of our relationship for seven days." You'll not want to discuss breaking up while "crazy" is still in control of the upset.

Frankly, it's wise to pre-plan a formal breakup strategy addressing both Master's and slave's needs. The document would discuss property division as well as protocols and rituals for recovering from the breakup's emotional trauma. Ritual will help, here. You'll want to take the time to identify the different emotions that hit you. The better you can understand the triggers, the better able you will be to disarm them for this or future relationships.

As Sergeant Major recommends, your best preparation is to develop protocols to cover HALT moments. HALT moments are those when you are:
- hungry/hurting;
- angry;
- lonely/loopy for some reason;
- tired.

I'll leave this section on specialized communication with a thought: To honor someone who is speaking, stop, focus on them, adopt the point of view that you are hunting for hidden treasures in their words. Be interested, not interesting. They're on stage, not you.

Follow those guides and a lot of your communication issues will melt away.

Using ceremony for stability

I understand there are rather polar ways of approaching M/s relationships; the organic method and the structured method. I also understand those who fall more on the organic side of the divide tend not to use formal protocols in their daily lives. While I have no idea how one would determine whether one approach is better or worse than the other, I fall solidly in the "highly structured" group. Speaking from that point of view, I've personally found protocols, rituals, and ceremonies to be extremely helpful in stabilizing my M/s relationships.

In this world, people create their own Path. Some people work very hard to make their lives magical; others let life happen and then react. As my Owner mentioned one time, you have to make the mundane aspects of life into something *special* or your life remains mundane. You get to *special* through ceremony. You create a *ceremony* by combining interrelated protocols focused on achieving a particular *purpose*. So: if your purpose is "to connect emotionally each evening," you build a ceremony around that. If your purpose is "to have outrageous sexual experiences," then you build a ceremony around your sex practices. If you want to make "bathing" special, you create bathing rituals.

Ceremonies and protocols help both Master and slave remain in their correct head space. Since it's up to Master to determine what is meant by "correct head space," it's also up to Master to create the physical and psychological conditions to get both of you there. Rituals, protocols, and hierarchy can all be used to keep your M/s relationship from drifting back to vanilla/mundane.

Since I've written this book for those experienced in M/s relationships, I'll assume you already know quite a bit about constructing protocols. If you wish a refresher, I'd send you back to one of my earlier books, *Protocol Handbook for the Leather slave: Theory and Practice.* Beyond that, I'd like to make a few quick points.

Clarify your protocols
Undoubtedly, you have a lot of things in your life you want done in a certain way. It's a bonding exercise simply to discuss these preferences. On the pragmatic side, stable relationships result from happy Masters

and happy slaves. There is another side to developing protocols to please Master: Master in turn praises and affirms the slave's service.

Along these same lines, written protocols represent a pathway to create *defined, repeatable processes.* It's rather like eating a hamburger at a national restaurant chain: you know exactly what you're going to get whether the restaurant is in Maine or Arizona. Such consistency comes from command-and-control. Managers, order-takers, cooks, and cashiers follow rigid protocols and the results are profitably consistent.

This applies directly to M/s relationships: Master needs both command and control. If Master has only *command,* result from orders will be random, undefined. "Get me a hamburger" will result in a randomly prepared piece of ground beef. If Master cares how the hamburger tastes, Master is going to have to execute *control* over how the hamburger is prepared. As M/s is based on command-and-control, Master can express *control* as a list of steps to follow to prepare hamburgers. Voila, a protocol for preparing hamburger.

By extrapolation, Master may have a preference for how that hamburger is served. Paper plate? Bone china? Dimmed lights? In front of the TV? All these choices are subject to protocols for the purpose of.... well, that's why you have to prepare your own protocols. Your purpose and my purpose are not likely to coincide at this level of personal preference.

> You have to make the mundane special or it's just mundane. You get to "special" through protocols.
>
> —Jen

Chapter 5: Little bits of ideas

Yes, slave serves Master. However, Master must also sleep sometime. Master may feel the need to be served in certain ways, but the solution must also fall within slave's skills, knowledge, and capabilities. Protocols result from devising strategies that meet your needs.

Protocols do much more than specify rules for slave's behavior; they help to keep the relationship from drifting back to vanilla. Protocols represent the moment-by-moment bond that reminds each of you that this is a very special Path. Along these lines, and realizing many readers have been in their relationship for decades, if you don't already use speech, walking, and dining protocols, I'd strongly encourage you to develop some. It's not my place to suggest specifics; my role is only to make general observations. If you're interested in reviewing basic protocols with the intent of modifying them to suit your situation, I'd refer you to my book: *Protocols for the Leather slave: Handbook of theory and practice.*

Clearly, protocol preferences differ between people. The ways we want our slaves to do things will vary to the extent we have different skills and personal preferences. Bottom line: how you want your slave to behave around you is an outgrowth of your values, and your values are an outgrowth of your experiences.

Epilogue

There you have it. You've finished the book.

Before you leave, I thought I'd offer some summary points. These are only my opinions and should be taken as no more than that. Some of these are from earlier chapters; others are being added as I type.

I'll start by agreeing that I have a point of view. I'll also agree that my point of view is an acquired taste and flow from my life experiences. Understandingly, it's taken me years of study to develop this outlook. It's taken lots of reading, lots of M/s trial and error, and lots of counseling. My views have also been strongly shaped from discussions with people like you, whom I've met in classes and presentations I've been giving since 2007.

That said, here are some thoughts.

I absolutely believe that participating in a structured relationship can be a pathway to a magical future. For many of us, it's a kind of second chance at life; it's a way of living *differently*. Speaking personally, I've been able to maneuver through life more efficiently and effectively in a structured relationship than I did in my marriages of 17 and 14 years.

All personal paths differ to some degree, even though most of us lead lives largely circumscribed by our Western culture and American society. We all have to work through common impediments to find our own path. For example, we all lead very busy lives, although the busyness is largely meaningless in the end. We also are encouraged to be distracted from thinking. TV is so accessible; sports events are so exciting. Tabloids encourage us to concern ourselves with the lives of people we don't even know. Our lives are filled with easy and interesting *things to do.* Reading, discussion, and introspection are sent to the back of the room.

Yet, within the M/s community there are many who do, in fact, study ways to use focus and mindfulness to maintain the purpose of their relationship. Many have learned how to maintain their relationship's purpose through clarity of intent. Every so often, you see a couple that has figured out how to build a symbiotic relationship; a relationship in which they accomplish more spectacular results as a couple than either person could obtain individually. For these people, the relationship, itself, takes on its own power.

Because there are no set models (customary ways of behaving) for authority-imbalanced structures, you can use your M/s life to recreate yourselves. You don't have to be who you've been. You can choose differently.

Under Master's guidance, you each have the opportunity to change those aspects of who you were to become the person you secretly wished to be. Have you longed to be a stronger leader or better communicator? Have you wanted to improve negotiation or problem-solving skills? Now, you have the opportunity to remake your world so it aligns with your dreams.

While complex, M/s relationships can be a sophisticated way to be very clear about what you want for yourself and your partner—accompanied by a plan of action. No, not everybody takes advantage of these aspects of a structured relationship, but not everybody takes advantage of *anything.*

In an M/s dynamic, Master has a highly prized asset: a slave. The slave represents wealth. Some people are able to make wealth grow; some people go bankrupt. Money doesn't "grow" without management and care; a slave's value depends largely upon Master's ability to manage it. That's where wisdom, empathy, and vision come into play.

One cannot do Mastery casually. One cannot do slave casually. Mastery requires time and application. Not to put anyone on the spot, but if you are away from one another during the day, come home to kids or to television, eat unceremoniously, go to bed, wake up and repeat the process, how do you get to mastery? Either you are working on the relationship or you're not really *in* the relationship.

My own approach to this conundrum has been to make daily tasks into something *special* to avoid being overwhelmed by the boringly mundane aspects of life. Invite beauty and passion into your life. Find things you love doing and do them well. Build protocols to turn the common into the uncommon. Build rituals out of your protocols: imbue the rituals with meaning that become part of who you are as a couple. Formal speech and position protocols can become your allies. They are a moment-by-moment visible and auditory reminder of both the power imbalances and also of the special nature of your relationship. You bathe each day: how about building bathing rituals? You both eat dinner: how about building a ceremony celebrating yourselves as a couple before you begin to eat.

Oh, and while we're near the topic, your clothing matters. The way you dress affects the way you behave. That's why private schools have uniforms and why businessmen wear suits, right? When you get home from work (or on weekend evenings when you are planning on doing something together), consider changing your clothes. Consider playing dress-up and have a lovely dinner in your own home. You don't have to own sterling silver or bone china to create elegance; elegance comes from your imagination and is driven by your intent. If your combined purpose is to make the evening special, it will be so.

Over the years, I've learned how important it is to act deliberately on

Chapter 5: Little bits of ideas

the knowledge that today is the only "today" that ever will be. No other day will be quite the same. Since our days are comprised of our choices, it's pretty easy to see how our choices are working out. We have only to look back to last week, last month or last year and our choices are vividly revealed. Unfortunately, it can sometimes be a challenge to figure out what you'd like to change in the upcoming weeks, months or years to avoid living a lifetime of similar experiences. That's where introspection and close communication with your partner get involved. Interestingly, this is also the point at which gratitude takes on an important role. Actively practicing gratitude strongly influences one's world view. However, I'm drifting away from the main point, so it's time to move on.

Now: I realize that many couples "do M/s" without much (or any) ceremony or discussion. I realize that many couples come home to a house that is a wreck: they are working their asses off just to survive. By day's end they are so exhausted they don't have the energy to do much. At least not today. But, every journey starts with a first step. What can you do right now? Clean up the kitchen? Straighten your closets? Identify the purpose of your relationship? Stop smoking? Exercise? Volunteer in your community? Set an example?

I'll admit, I'm not sure how I would have reacted to the material in this epilogue if I were reading it at age 30 or 45 or even 55. However, I'm not 30 or 45 or 55; I'm 70. It takes time for some of life's truths to make sense.

So: this is where I'll leave you. Jen and I wish you well on your Journey and will try to help you if you contact us.

Once more I suggest: if you can possibly afford to do so, become certified as a Master Practitioner NLP coach. This one act will transform your work life and your relationships. It will give you a different future.

Good night.

Dr. Bob and M. Jen

Supplements

Supplement A: Acknowledgements

- **Master Michael**, (2014 International Master) was tremendously helpful as the final reader. He pointed out a number of areas that needed tightening and better flow and (as you have read) made many comments that I have included throughout the book. Thank you VERY much for taking your time to do such an outstanding job. (Facebook: Michael Chgo; Fetlife: MasterMichael_S)

- **Dan** made the first content edit. That's an heroic task, for my "raw" writing can be hard to follow. Dan identified many areas that needed serious reworking. Dan, thank you for your thoughtful comments. I believe that I took them all. (Fetlife: AngelRiot)

- **Nikita** was able to make a number of very helpful comments towards the end of the editing process, particularly in the first part of the book. For some reason, the first parts of all my books have been particularly difficult for me. I think it has to do with catching the flow of the book. Thank you, again, for reading through it and smoothing it even more. (Fetlife: Miss_Kita)

Supplement B: A Special Glossary of terms

Every once in a while—practically never, actually—I discover explanations of things (or interpretations of things) particularly well developed and expressed yet slightly *off* or *different from* the way I look at things. This is the case with Al Turtle's parsing of some common words from our Master/slave culture.

This is a glossary of terms developed by Al Turtle and published on his website www.alturtle.com. Al has been kind enough to permit me to reprint his material. I've lightly edited a few of his points so the phrasing is congruent with my writing style. The ideas remain his—and for the most part, I agree with him. I think these are very clever and I particularly like Al's humor.

A Good Idea: something you decide to do today, and next week you look back and still think it was a good Idea.

Agreement:
- A mythical state in which multiple people's viewpoints are the same.
- A decision by all parties that their view on a topic seems close enough to proceed to action.

Anger: a general term for one of the two survival emotions and one of the four prime emotions in humans, characterized by an increase of nor-epinephrine in the bloodstream. While it may be stronger or less strong, it is usually indicated by the presence of fighting behavior, and is frequently accompanied by the emotions of *fear* or *fleeing*, and by the behaviors of *freezing* or *submitting*. Its general function is to raise general energy levels to assist in pushing through frustrating blocks.

Argument:
- The act of two people who are using "military think" to try to persuade the other to conform with their point of view.
- A situation where two people are trying to be Master at the same time and both are using a *punishment system* to coerce the other into silence and the appearance of agreement.
- The actions of two bullies.
- The verbal form of physical fighting. This is also referred to as *verbal battery*. An indicator of an unstable Master/slave

structure.

Autonomy: The state of humans in which their actions are a result both of external input and internal reflection. All human action begins in their head. Our actions and reactions are our choices: *autonomy* represents the comfortable awareness of this condition. This is a conscious characteristic of "Dialogical Thinking."

BCR: Short for **B**ehavior **C**hange **R**equest. An articulated request by your partner to change certain specific acts in ways that would contribute to healing some of the wounds you are repeatedly inflicting on them.

Biological Dream: A summary of the collective drives that characterize all human yearning. Awakened at birth, the Biological Dream is reawakened by *romantic love*, frustrated in the resulting *power struggles of relationships*, and finally realized in *vintage love* (e.g., love that has endured past ten years).

Boundary: a virtual line between that which belongs to one person and that which belongs to another.

Boundary Invasion: The other person's behavior that triggers an emotional upset in the responding person.

Boundary Skills: The ability to clearly define and defend your boundaries. All boundary skills are defensive.

Bully: A person who wants their way and when they don't get their way, they make other people unhappy.

Caring Behavior: Any behavior that successfully communicates the presence of safety to your partner's "Lizard Brain." Alternately any behavior that enables them to feel loved or cared for; nurtured.

Couples' Dialogue (Intentional Dialogue): A skill-training tool (part of *Imago Relationships Training*), consisting of three steps that essentially translate as: *mirroring, validating*, and *empathizing*.

Dialogical: Peacefully sharing points of view.

Dialogical Thinking: The habit of thinking that there is no specific (or correct) view of reality and that each person behaves congruently within the context of their own realities. Dialogical thinking assumes that people continuously revise and improve their viewpoints and act consistent with their understanding of reality at any given time. This form of thinking also assumes that others can either share their viewpoints or keep it hidden from others.

Dialogue: A symptom of Dialogical Thinking.
- Any sentence that implies the existence of multiple points of view of reality.
- A conversation in which both are comfortably sharing their differing ways of seeing and appreciating the world.

Dialogical Resilience: A durable skill and habit of remaining in, and maintaining, dialogical space even when others revert to non-dialogical speaking or behavior.

Diversity: The state of humans to experience reality uniquely and the comfortable awareness of this characteristic. People act, think, and speak based on their experiences. This is a conscious characteristic of Dialogical Thinking.

Dysfunctional: Something that you are doing that is leading you away from your own goal.

Emotion: An event in the body that includes time duration, intensity, the factor of awareness, accurate or inaccurate labeling, and social values of "good" or "bad." As distinct from cognition, emotions occur simultaneously with thinking and are part of each person's experience.

Empathy: The ability to relate to (and understand) the inner world of another as different from your own inner world.

Fair: A situation where two or more people believe that things are evenly balanced using a win/win model. It is never fair when one person thinks it fair and the other does not. Fairness is established when each person would be willing to take the other person's "deal."

Fear: Characterized by increased adrenaline in the blood, *fear* is a general term referring to one of the prime human emotions. While it may vary in intensity, fear is usually expressed by one or more of three instinctive behaviors: fleeing, freezing, or submitting. *Fear* is usually present when *fighting* behavior is triggered. Fear's general function is to alert the individual to threats to their survival and to enable defensive responses.

Fleeing: A survival behavior initiated by your Lizard Brain and characterized by visibly moving away from or limiting contact with the threatening person or environment.

Freezing: A survival behavior initiated by your Lizard Brain and characterized by invisibility (e.g., "laying low"). When one "freezes" in this context, not only do you not move, but your breathing rhythm also changes.

Grief: One of the prime emotions in humans, characterized by an increased flow of prolactin in the brain. Its general function is to adjust a human to the experience of loss.

Guilt: The fear that someone is going to punish you for something you did in the past. Guilt is based on time travel: it's putting today's wisdom into yesterday's event. (By the way, only your enemies benefit from your feelings of guilt, for those emotions keep you from attaining your potential. It's your potential greatness that triggers envy and jealousy in others.)

Healing: Any action that has the effect of resolving a wound and removing the survival habits that have become associated with that wound.

Invalidation: Any experience of feeling misunderstood. This word can describe the behavior that triggers the feeling.

Joy: Characterized by an increased endorphin release in the brain, *joy* is a general term representing one of the prime emotions in humans. In a general sense, *joy* rewards you for accomplishing something that is congruent with your personal goals in life.

Listening: Putting energy into consciously hearing another person's verbal and non-verbal communications.

Lie: To knowingly leave someone in a state of misunderstanding about something you believe is important to them. *Active lying* is to say something that is not so; *passive lying* is to leave unsaid something that you know is important to someone.

Master Position: Maintaining control in relationships by defining reality while simultaneously coercing silence from others.

Master/slave: A posture of relating to others that assumes the primacy of one point of view over another. This includes two skills: the *truth system* and the *punishment system*. This posture is functional when:
- the task at hand requires it,
- property ownership is involved, or
- in a group emergency.

Many believe that this posture is dysfunctional in all other situations. (But they're not reading this book, are they? RJR)

Master Talk: A symptom of *military thinking*. Any sentence that implies

Supplements

that there exists only one correct view of reality and that sends an implied threat to those who do not agree or who are not willing to conform.

Military Think: The habit of thinking as if there is only one correct view of reality. Seeking the "correct" view of reality. The tendency to get others to agree with (and to conform to) the stronger person's perspective while concurrently persuading others to keep their viewpoints hidden.

Mirroring: A skill-training tool (usually but not necessarily verbal), that make others feel heard.

Other-Esteem: A somewhat fragile tendency to like yourself or admire yourself if others like or admire you.

Panic: A physical state of tension characterized by reactivity that is initiated by the brain's survival mechanism—the Lizard Brain. This emotional state is visible and measurable, often characterized by such behaviors as fleeing, withdrawing, silence, distraction, inattention, submission and placating, or aggressive pushing and fighting. People move away from (and thereafter avoid) situations or people that cause them to feel panicky.

Passive Master: A person who wants control without responsibility. A person who uses passive punishment when they do not get their way, but do not articulate what it is that they want.

Patience: An adult skill of being relaxed and comfortable when events do not happen in the way (or at the rate) that they want.

Persuasion: An act of pre-invalidation where one person is attempting to pressure another into changing their view.

Power Struggle: A temporary period in a relationship characterized by increasing frustration and distress brought about by fruitless attempts to "recover a beautiful relationship" by using skills that not only do not work, but that actually increase the relationship distress. A time when couples use traditional relating skills in an attempt to achieve a "Biological Dream"-type relationship. This period occurs in all intimate relationships and is meant to end. For each couple the question is when to end it and whether to end it by:
- learning new skills,
- giving up the dream, or

- breaking up or divorcing.

Pre-Validate: The *attitude* of the awareness that people make sense before they open their mouths to tell about it, or the *action* of displaying the attitude of that awareness to another. A pre-judgment (expressed through one's actions), that people always think that they are making sense in their way of looking at the world.

Pulling: Any act that communicates an invitation to say more and to share more deeply. A "straight pull" communicates a simple invitation (e.g., "Go on.") A "deepening pull" communicates an invitation along with an area of interest to the pulling person (e.g., "Please share more what you mean by that word." or "Please share more about what led you to do that conclusion.")

Punishment System: A method of using threat of degradation or dismissal to extend the benefits of conformity. This is a normal feature of a Master/slave relationship.

Purpose: The word that we give to some internal drive to accomplish a specific (personally meaningful) life-task.

Relational Maturity: The skillful maintenance of your partner's needs for safety, belonging, diversity, autonomy, and purpose.

Reliable Membership: A need for adequate and reliable (but not excessive) connection with others of like mind. Excessive, unreliable, or inadequate connection triggers panic. Panic behaviors related to unreliable or inadequate connection manifest as clinging, pursuing, interrogating, and stalking. The panic behaviors related to excessive connection involve avoiding, withdrawing, isolating, and building interpersonal walls/barriers.

Resentment: The memory of past invalidation or a collection of such memories.

Romantic Love: A temporary state of awakened connection (sometimes called infatuation) that is an expression of deep yearning for the Biological Dream. It most commonly occurs when newly connecting with a partner, a lost family or family member, or a community of like-minded people.

Safe: A physical state of relaxation characterized by inactivity of the brain's survival mechanism—the Lizard Brain. This state is often characterized by play and fun, playful sex, nurturing, loving, and caring behaviors, or creative activities. People seek, move toward, and tend to remain in situations in which they feel safe.

Self-Esteem: A durable tendency to like and admire yourself for what you do and for what you are, even when others actively dislike you.

Sense: The combined factors within a person's being that results in the expression of their logically congruent actions.

Skill: An acquired action that requires learning and practice.

Slave Position: The tendency to submission, yielding control and responsibility to others. This is a boundary-less arrangement.

Submitting: A survival behavior initiated by the Lizard Brain and characterized by two steps:
- giving in, following other's orders, conforming, or letting the other think they are winning;
- the backlash or revenge that is the expression of resentment built during step one.

The Imago: A relatively durable and unique image of our childhood caretakers. This image is usually formed between the ages of three and seven, resonates with deep familiarity, and is the common basis for partner selection in romantic relationships. The Imago contains both desirable and problematical traits. It is the re-selection of a mate that exhibits the problematical traits of our childhood caretakers (usually parents) that brings about the uniquely difficult growth challenges experienced by married couples.

The Lizard Brain: This phrase refers to the primitive reptilian part of brains. It functions to guarantee a person's survival. Unfortunately, the Lizard Brain sometimes functions independently of our rational brain and can crudely initiate reactive behaviors that embarrass us once the triggering conditions are neutralized.

Truth: A subjective reality that all humans experience differently. Contact with reality filtered through the lens of our personal background and unique experiences.

Truth System: The process of determining the correct point of view by ignoring your own opinions on a subject and referring to (or substituting) the viewpoint of someone you consider to be in a superior position. This substitution of someone else's opinions over your own opinions occurs as you also ignore the viewpoints of others. This is a normal feature of a Master/slave relationship.

Tyrant Factor: The tendency to slip into Master behavior when confronted by the passive form of MasterTalk or with slave behavior.

Understand: To know something well enough to teach it to others.

Upset: A general term referring to the presence of emotions such as fear, anger, or grief.

Validate: To make a person feel understood. The visible (usually verbal) act of bearing witness to the logic of their thoughts or actions.

Victimicity: The tendency to gain power (or comfort) by passing responsibility for your actions and decisions onto another.

Vintage Love: A relatively permanent state of relating and connected characterized by competence with Biological Dream skills, low stress, and a high sense of self and joint satisfaction.

Win-Loose: A relationship event where one or both believe the other is the only one getting their needs met.

Win-Win: A relationship event where both participants believe they are getting their needs met at the same time, cooperatively.

Working: Doing things you are not inclined to do. Learning new skills.

Wound: An emotional hole or emptiness that usually originated in childhood and has continued into adulthood. Wounds are usually characterized by upset, reactivity (often accompanied by blaming behavior), and declarations of unmet personal/ emotional needs. Some people consider emotional wounds to be "unfinished" conditions for which a person is currently seeking completion.

Wus Factor: The tendency to slide into the slave position when confronted with Master behavior.

Supplement C: My own definitions of submissive and slave as used in this book

submissive: A person who chooses to submit to the will of their conditions. The conditions typically including terms of service, length of service, areas of the submissives' life the dominant does not get to control, the hard and soft limits when they play or just interact, and the safewords they will use when scening. Although it is counterintuitive, the submissive has (through safewords) some degree of control over an sm play scene—at least until they enter subspace and don't have much to say about anything.

Some typical characteristics of the submissive's role:

- D/s relationships are usually based on power *exchange.* This means the submissive—who normally has a certain amount of personal authority over what they, themselves, may or may not do or have done to them—can give that personal authority to the D-type for a prescribed period in exchange for specifically negotiated benefits.
- Submissives have a strong desire to serve, but their service is limited to their Dom/me and is offered with specific negotiated conditions.
- Typically, the negotiated area includes the submissive's terms of service, the length of that service, the hard and soft limits, and both physical and emotional safewords.
- The submissive will also negotiate certain aspects of their life that the Dom doesn't control, such as the submissive's biological family and children, work, education, and religious observance.
- The conditions under which the submissive is willing to serve can be renegotiated. (This is a major issue: the submissive retains the personal authority to ask their Dominant to renegotiate their terms of service, but the Dominant is under no obligation to accept the newly proposed conditions.)
- While an sm play scene would not necessarily end if the D-type violates the s-type's hard limits, if the breach is severe, the s-type may view the transgression as a breach of the fundamental *relationship* trust, and end the relationship. I know of two such cases.
- The Dom/me may be permitted to break "soft limits" (things the submissive has said they really aren't interested in) after discussing it with the submissive and obtaining their permission.
- In many/most cases, submissives cross back and forth between retaining and surrendering control over some aspect of their lives and continue to make decisions in the areas off-limits for

their Dom/me
- A submissive re-submits to the Dom at the start of any scene or activity over which the Dom/me has negotiated authority. Importantly, the submissive retains the choice as to whether or not to submit to the Dom/me.

slave: A person who has transferred authority over him/herself to another. In a general sense, the distinction between a *submissive* and *slave* focuses on whether someone retains any personal authority and/or retains any meaningful decision-making capabilities or surrenders that authority to someone else. Additionally, play rules are usually different for slaves, as they lack the authority to tell their Master to stop a scene.

Some typical characteristics of a consensual slave's role:
- M/s relationships are based on *authority transfer*. At least in theory, this means that once the slave-candidate has, in fact, surrendered personal authority over him/herself to their Master/ Owner, they may no longer make personal decisions about most things, including whom they may contact and befriend.
- The core values are *service* and *obedience*, and the s-type's act of "showing up" day after day constitutes ongoing consent.
- The word "no" takes on some function of meaning because Master cannot function if command authority is questioned. (In the Military, a court-marshal pursuant to willfully violating the Military Code of Conduct represents a parallel situation.) An act of willfulness by slave can certainly terminate a relationship.*
- As "chattel slavery" is illegal in Western civilization, we recognize the slave always has the option of actually saying "no" to its Master, although that "no" may terminate the relationship. As Master Michael notes: "It might not be just willfulness; it could represent a serious breakdown of the relationship where the slave is exercising a human right to protect themselves."
- As a slave cannot "red out," slave has implicitly accepted their Master's limits and does what is asked of them regardless of their feelings about it. ("What does 'liking it' have to do with it?")
- The Master determines what rights the slave has to personal property and what access/use slave has of monies it previously

owned or earned.
- A slave's purpose is to make Master's life easier. In that regard, a slave is expected to know Master's wants and likes in order to take independent action (such as grocery or clothes shopping) on Master's behalf. This demonstrates proactive rather than reactive service and is intended to demonstrate slaves initiative as a thinking person.
- A slave may be more interested in taking care of others ("service heart") than in being taken care of ("sorts by others" vs. "sorts by self" in psychology-speak).
- A slave may very well be dominant in most other aspects of their life, but choose to be submissive to (or simply to serve) one single person.

* Note: In a general way, the slave is not "allowed" to use the word "no" because that word expresses willfulness, and one of the core purposes of the M/s structure is that Master controls slave's will. In lieu or saying "no," slave may say, "Sir, if it pleases you, Sir" (to mean: "Master, I really rather would not do that and of course I'll do it.") or "Sir, only if it pleases you, Sir" (which is as close to "no" as most slaves are permitted). Note: Master may ethically push through an "only if" reply so long as Master believes doing so is in the slave's best interest. Many believe that a Master who pushes their slave through an "only if" reply just because they have the authority to do so violates the basic pact between Master and slave and has committed a relationship-damaging breach of trust.

Supplement D: Stimulating/relevant web site links

- Very good list of suggested lifeskills: http://advancedlifeskills. com/blog/sitemap/
- Al Turtle's web site—filled with insightful observations and skills/techniques:
  http://www.alturtle.com/archives/category/main-page/ relationships/map-of-relationships
- Problems arising from structured relationships: http://www. bilerico.com/2013/04/power_problems_in_kink_bdsm_

relationships.php
- Twin Flame discussion: http://www.beautyandtruth.org/twin-flame-relationship.html

Supplement E: Reading suggestions

Books on self-evaluation and self-correction
- *Please Understand Me: Character and temperament types,* by David Keirsey and Marilyn Bates (Prometheus Nemesis Book Company) 1984
- *Please Understand Me II, temperament, character, intelligence* by David Keirsey (Prometheus Nemesis Book Company) 1984
- *Supercoach: 10 secretes to transform anyone's life* by Michael Neill (Hay House Publishers) 2009
- *How to See Yourself As You Really Are* by His Holiness the Dalai Lama (Atria Books) 2006
- *Light Emerging: The journey of personal healing* by Barbara Ann Brennan (Bantam Books) 1993
- *Mind Over Mood: Change how you feel by changing the way you think* by Dennis Greenberger, Ph.D. and Christine Padesky, Ph.D.
- *What to Say when you Talk to Your Self* by Shad Helmstetter (Pocket Books) 1982

Books about asking questions or learning styles
- *Leading with Questions* by Michael Marquardt (Jossey-Bass) 2005
- *Learning Styles: Reaching everyone God gave you to teach* by Marlene D. LeFever (David Cook Publishing Co.) 1995
- *What Every Body is Saying* by Joe Navarro (Collins Living, an imprint of HarperCollins Publishers) 2008
- *Crucial Conversations Tools for Talking when stakes are high* by Kerry Patterson, Ron McMillan, and Al Switzler (McGraw Hill) 2002
- *Living in Gratitude: a journey that will change your life* by Angeles Arrien (Sounds True, Inc.) 2011

Books about focus and mindfulness
- *Focusing* by Eugene T. Gendlin, Ph.D. (A Bantam New Age

Book)1981
- *How to Train a Wild Elephant, and other adventures in mindfulness* by Jan Chozen Bays, M.D. (Shambhala Press) 2011
- *Just One Thing: developng a buddha brain one simple practice at a time* by Rick Hanson (New Harbinger Publications) 2011
- *The Practicing Mind: developing focus and discipline in your life* by Thomas M. Sterner (New World Library) 2012

Supplement F: About the authors

Robet J. Rubel, Ph.D.

Robert Rubel (Dr. Bob), author, educator and photographer is an educational sociologist and researcher by training. He currently has ten books in print and two DVDs (Books: four on Master/slave topics, two on advanced sex techniques, one on fire play, and three erotic art photo books. DVDs: fire play and beginning impact play).

Recipient of the 2008 Pantheon of Leather's Community Choice Award (man), Dr. Bob has been involved in the BDSM and Total Power Exchange (TPE) scene since the summer of 2001, throwing himself into the literature of the field as though it were an academic study. He presents, judges, and sells his books at weekend kink conferences throughout the year.

Now starting in on his 70s, Bob has had three long-term relationships: a 17-year marriage, a 14-year marriage, and a 10-year Owner/

property relationship in which after two years his Owner gave him his own slave. The three of them remained together for eight more years. In his current relationship he serves Jen, his Master.

M. Jen Fairfield

Jen is Dr. Bob's Master. She has extensive experience managing authority-imbalanced relationships. Her D/s experience began in 1992 as she dipped her toe in the water with a nurturing Mommy/boy relationship. Seeking more control than the Mommy/boy relationship could offer, Jen ended that relationship after one year and—following a year of introspection and personal clarification—entered a full-blown D/s relationship that she ran for another 16 years.

Jen found her home in the Leather culture in the fall of 2010 and has embraced her calling as a Leather woman—to live a highly focused life with a partner (or partners) who are willing to hold themselves to exacting moral and ethical standards.

Over the past three years, Jen has been attending conferences and workshops, reading books, and working closely with Dr. Bob, as he has been researching and writing books and making presentations all over the US and Canada. Over the last year, Jen has developed a growing number of presentations that are separate from Bob's.

Supplement G: Other Books by Robert J. Rubel and M. Jen Fairfield

All existing and future publications by Robert J. Rubel, Ph.D. and M. Jen Fairfield can be purchased through Amazon or though our website www.KinkMastery.com

Books on Master/slave Relations

Master/slave Mastery: Updated handbook of concepts, approaches, and practices
This book is the first in a series of books devoted to Master/slave topics. It is designed to give you a thorough understanding not only the intricacies of authority-imbalanced relationships, but also how vastly different M/s structures are from D/s structures. This series of books are designed both to demystify this topic and to give you the tools and knowledge to explore this small sub-culture that lives within the overall BDSM culture. By Robert J. Rubel and M. Jen Fairfield (2014).

Master/slave Relations: Handbook of Theory and Practice
This book by Robert Rubel was totally revised and is now available as: *Master/slave Mastery: Updated handbook of*

concepts, approaches, and practices, listed immediately above.

Protocol Handbook for the Leather slave: Theory and Practice
This is the gender-neutral version of *Protocols: Handbook for the Female slave*. More than a book of traditional Leather protocols, this book demonstrates how to use protocols to make your particular relationship magical. This book is intended to suggest protocols that you, yourself, will adapt to your particular structure.

Master/slave Relations: Communications 401 – the advanced course
All relationships have communication challenges, and many of these challenges are amplified when living in a structured relationship. This book teases out some of communication glitches that are often hard to identify and modify even in vanilla relationships. This book is written specifically for couples living in a D/s or M/s structure where there are certain constraints when speaking with one another.

Master/slave Relations: Solutions 402 – living in harmony
If you're sensing that one of you is growing apart from the other, if you are concerned that one or more of your *core values* may be different from your partner and you want to work on growing back together, this is your book. It's really a book of *things to think/talk about* that will strengthen your relationship.

Books on BDSM by Robert Rubel and M. Jen Fairfield
BDSM Mastery—Basics: your guide to play, parties, and scene protocols.
This is not a book that explains what BDSM is, this is a book that explains what BDSM is all about. This is a book for people who are considering stepping into real time BDSM, and it is also a book for people who have been involved in the community for a while and know enough to appreciate how all the little bits of information they've picked up all nest together.

This book treats the world of BDSM as a culture unto itself and goes a long way to explaining the expectations, rules, and words that are common to this culture.

This book does *not* tell you how to use any implements (floggers, canes, etc), but it does explain why in the world you'd want to use such implements.

BDSM Mastery—Relationships: a guide for creating mindful relationships for Dominants and submissives
This is a book about relationships. Adventuresome relationships. Relationships that are not exactly like *vanilla* relationships— traditional relationships as practiced by the average person you'd meet at a baseball game. BDSM relationships differ in two specific ways: first, they usually involve a power-imbalanced structure (one person is clearly in charge and the other person is clearly following); second, the kind of sex that adventuresome folks practice is, well, *not vanilla.*

Biases though I am, I'd say that if you're in any way involved with BDSM and considering taking a partner, you'll find this book very useful. It can save both D-types and s-types a lot of heartache and anger.

Books Other BDSM Topics
- *Flames of Passion: Handbook of Erotic Fire Play* Las Vegas: Nazca Plains, 2006.

SMTech Book+DVD Combinations
- *Fire Play: A Safety Training Course* (70-minute DVD plus 48-page book) Las Vegas: Nazca Plains, 2012
- *Impact Play 101: Building Your Skills* (70-minute DVD plus 48-page book) Las Vegas: Nazca Plains, 2012

Books on Advanced Sexual Practices
Squirms, Screams, and Squirts: Handbook for going from great sex to extraordinary sex

Most men want to be good lovers. Most men want to please their female partners. Unfortunately, exactly how to please a female lover is a mystery to many men—and good instruction is very difficult to find. In fact, I wrote this book because I was not satisfied with the books that I *could* find on the subject. Here, in this one volume, is absolutely first-rate information about *the who, what, where, when, why,* and *how* of creating an intensely pleasurable sexual experience for a woman.

Squirms, Screams, and Squirts: The Workbook
This is a companion book to *Squirms, Screams, and Squirts,* and is intended to get the two of you talking about areas you seldom discuss even though you've been together forever. There are lots of "fill-in-the-blank" and checklist pages, but the overall intent is to get you thinking *differently* about sex.

Screams of Pleasure: Guide for Extraordinary Sex for those with Erectile Dysfunction
(Slightly revised version of Squirms, Screams, and Squirts) (2009)

Books of Erotic and Fetish Art
Three books on erotic and fetish photography titled (with an eye towards perverse humor) were published by the Nazca Plains Corp (Las Vegas) 2006.
- *Parts: The Erotic Photographic Art of Robert J. Rubel, PhD.*
- *Wholes: The Erotic Photographic Art of Robert J. Rubel, PhD.*
- *Holes: The Erotic Photographic Art of Robert J. Rubel, PhD.*

Edited Publications
Bob served as the Managing Editor of **Power Exchange Magazine** in 2007-2008. Issue Themes
- *Master/slave Relations—male Master*
- *Master/slave Relations—female Master*
- *Bootblacking*
- *FemDomme*
- *Pony Play*
- *Polyamory*

- *Daddy/boy*
- *Leather Spirituality*
- *Pup/Trainer*

In 2007 Rubel made a marketing decision and transformed *Power Exchange Magazine* and into a small book format. This series, *Power Exchange Books' Resource Series,* are 100-page books on focused topics of interest to BDSM or Leather folk. The series is about the "why" of what we do, not the "how." Book titles include:
- *Playing with Disabilities*
- *The Art of Slavery* edited by salve laura
  One often hears: *"It's easier said than done."* This is certainly true of the art of slave service. This is a delightful collection of nine essays written by established slaves who offer readers a glimpse into the world that they have created with their Masters.
- *Protocols: A Variety of Views*
  This is a collection of essays by nine senior Masters or slaves about how they use protocols in their own relationship.
- *Rope, Bondage, and Power*
- *Age Play*

Made in the USA
San Bernardino,
CA